Basic Math

G.A.M.E.S.

Games, Activities, and More to Educate Students

Math

Kindergarten

by
Lynette Pyne

Carson-Dellosa Publishing Company, Inc.
Greensboro, North Carolina

Basic Math

G.A.M.E.S.

Games, Activities, and More to Educate Students

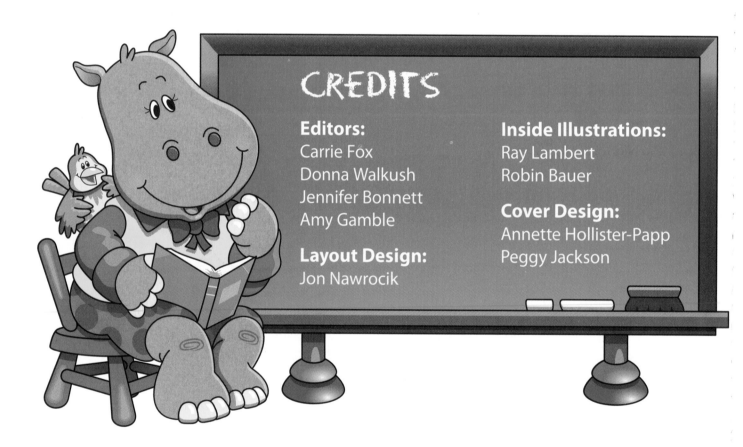

CREDITS

Editors:
Carrie Fox
Donna Walkush
Jennifer Bonnett
Amy Gamble

Layout Design:
Jon Nawrocik

Inside Illustrations:
Ray Lambert
Robin Bauer

Cover Design:
Annette Hollister-Papp
Peggy Jackson

Printed in the USA • All rights reserved.   ISBN 1-59441-481-5

Table of Contents

How Do I Play? (game instructions)

Let's Play! (game materials)

I Played and I Conquered! (worksheets and assessments)

Introduction

How to Use the Games:

- *Basic Math G.A.M.E.S.* can be used to reinforce skills that students have been taught through the classroom curriculum.
- The games are an excellent tool for teaching students how to make independent choices and work on their own.
- Teach students how to cooperate and work in small groups using the games.

How to Make the Games:

- Assemble the games by attaching the student directions and title pieces to the appropriate containers. Then, laminate and cut out the color game pieces.
- *Basic Math G.A.M.E.S.* contain all of the game pieces you need to make each game, plus two worksheets for reinforcing and extending skills.

How to Display and Store the Games:

- Save space by hanging a clothesline under a chalkboard, bulletin board, or in a classroom corner. Use clothespins to display the games.
- Designate a shelf or table for the *Basic Math G.A.M.E.S.* Provide all of the materials students will need to complete the games in this area.
- As new skills are introduced, add or remove various *Basic Math G.A.M.E.S.* from the display area. Store the games in a plastic container or box when not in use.

How to Play the Games:

- Model how to play each game for the whole class before displaying it. Be sure to explain how students can play the games alone and in small groups.
- Explain and demonstrate required student behavior while using the games. Practice using normal speaking voices and show students how to quietly gather their materials and move from game to game.
- Announce when there is five minutes left until cleanup. Practice with the class what is expected during cleanup (quietly put away materials, place completed worksheets in the proper place, and return the games to the correct area).
- Provide a box or folder where students can turn in completed "Look What I Learned" and "On My Own" worksheets.

How Do I Play?

Cookie Count

Skill: Counting Up to 30

How to Make the Game:

1. Laminate and cut out the title piece, student instructions, game board, number cards, and cookie cards (pages B1–B6).
2. Attach the title piece and the student instructions to the front of a file folder.
3. Tape or glue the two halves of the cookie jar game board together and tape the entire game board to the inside of the folder.
4. Place the cookie cards and number cards in labeled envelopes and attach to the back of the folder with a paper clip.
5. Place copies of the "Look What I Learned" and the "On My Own" worksheets inside the folder.

How to Play the Game:

Have the student choose a number card and place it at the top of the cookie jar game board. Then, she should count the matching number of cookies and place them in the jar. The student should check her work by turning over the number card to reveal the correct number of cookies. Play continues until cookies have been counted for each number card.

Up, Up, and Away

Skill: Matching Numbers to Number Words

How to Make the Game:

1. Laminate and cut out the title piece, student instructions, and game pieces (pages B7–B12).
2. Attach the title piece and the student instructions to the front of a large, resealable bag.
3. Place the game pieces and copies of the "Look What I Learned" and the "On My Own" worksheets inside the bag.

How to Play the Game:

Have the student choose a balloon and read the number word. Then, she should find the basket with the matching number and place it below the correct balloon. Play continues until each balloon has been matched with the correct basket. The student should check her work by turning over each basket to reveal the correct number word.

Count the Jelly Beans

Skill: Adding Sets Up to 10

How to Make the Game:

1. Laminate and cut out the title piece, student instructions, and game pieces (pages B13–B16).
2. Attach the title piece and the student instructions to the front of a large, resealable bag.
3. Place the game pieces and copies of the "Look What I Learned" and the "On My Own" worksheets inside the bag.

How to Play the Game:

Have the student choose a jelly bean problem card and count the jelly beans in each set. Then, he should add the sets and find the matching jelly bean jar card with the correct answer. Finally, the student should find the matching number problem card. Play continues until each jelly bean problem has been solved and matched to a number problem. The student should check his work by turning over each number problem card to see the matching jelly bean problem on the back.

Buzzing About

Skill: Subtraction Up to 10

How to Make the Game:

1. Laminate and cut out the title piece, student instructions, beehive game board, subtraction problems cards, bee cards, and answer cards (pages B17–B20).
2. Attach the title piece and the student instructions to the front of a file folder.
3. Tape or glue the beehive game board to the right inside section of the file folder.
4. Place the bee cards, problem cards, and answer cards in labeled envelopes and attach to the left inside section of the folder with a paper clip.
5. Place copies of the "Look What I Learned" and "On My Own" worksheets inside the folder.

How to Play the Game:

Have the student choose a problem card. She should place the number of bees indicated by the first number "inside" the beehive. Then, she should take the number of bees indicated by the second number back out of the beehive. Next, the student should count the number of bees left inside the beehive, find the matching answer card, and place it beside the problem card to show the completed problem. The student should check her work by turning over each problem card to see the correct answer. Play continues until each problem has been solved.

Doggone Fun!

Skill: Positional Words

How to Make the Game:

1. Laminate and cut out the title piece, student instructions, dog picture cards, and bone cards (pages B21–B24). Note: Do not cut out each individual dog picture. Instead, keep each horizontal pair together.
2. Attach the title piece and the student instructions to the front of a large mailing envelope.
3. Place the dog picture cards, bone cards, and copies of the "Look What I Learned" and the "On My Own" worksheets inside the envelope.

How to Play the Game:

Have the student choose a picture card. She should find the word that tells about each picture on the card. Play continues until the pictures on each card have been matched with the correct positional words. The student should check her work by turning over each picture card to see the correct positional words.

Shape Up

Skill: Sorting Shapes

How to Make the Game:

1. Laminate and cut out the title piece, student instructions, game mats, and picture cards (pages B25–B32).
2. Attach the title piece and the student instructions to the front of a large mailing envelope.
3. Place the game mats, picture cards, and copies of the "Look What I Learned" and the "On My Own" worksheets inside the envelope.

How to Play the Game:

Have the student choose a picture and place it on the correct game mat. Play continues until each picture card has been placed on the correct mat. The student should check his work by turning over each picture card to reveal the correct shape name.

Pretty Patchwork

Skill: Patterns

How to Make the Game:

1. Laminate and cut out the title piece, student instructions, pattern strips, and colorful squares (pages B33–B38).
2. Attach the title piece and the student instructions to the front of a large mailing envelope.
3. Place the pattern strips, colorful squares, and copies of the "Look What I Learned" and the "On My Own" worksheets inside the envelope.

How to Play the Game:

Have the student choose a pattern strip. Then, he should select the correct colorful squares to continue the pattern as far as possible. Play continues until each pattern has been continued. The student should check his work by placing each pattern strip below the colorful squares to see if they match.

Flower Power

Skill: Numerical Order Up to 10

How to Make the Game:

1. Laminate and cut out the title piece, student instructions, flower cards, and vase cards (pages B39–B41).
2. Attach the title piece and the student instructions to the front of a large, resealable bag.
3. Place the flower cards, vase cards, and copies of the "Look What I Learned" and "On My Own" worksheets inside the bag.

How to Play the Game:

Have the student put the vases in order from 1 to 10. Then, she should choose a flower card and count the flowers. The student should place the flowers "in" the correct vase. Play continues until each flower card has been matched to the correct vase. The student should check her work by turning over each flower card to reveal the number from the correct vase.

Monkey in the Middle

Skill: Numerical Order Up to 20

How to Make the Game:

1. Laminate and cut out the title piece, student instructions, monkey strips, and monkey cards (pages B42–B45).
2. Attach the title piece and the student instructions to the front of a large mailing envelope.
3. Place the monkey strips, monkey cards, and copies of the "Look What I Learned" and the "On My Own" worksheets inside the envelope.

How to Play the Game:

Have the student choose a monkey strip. He should find the monkey card that belongs in the empty space on the strip so that the numbers are in the correct order. Play continues until each monkey strip number sequence has been completed. The student should check his work by turning over each monkey card to see the matching shape from the empty space on the monkey strip. To extend this activity, have the student put all of the monkey strips and cards in the correct numerical order.

Gone Fishing

Skill: Comparing Sets of Objects

How to Make the Game:

1. Laminate and cut out the title piece, student instructions, fish cards, and word cards (pages B46–B49). Note: Do not cut out each individual fish set. Instead, keep each horizontal pair of sets together.
2. Attach the title piece and the student instructions to the front of a large, resealable bag.
3. Place the fish cards, word cards, and copies of the "Look What I Learned" and the "On My Own" worksheets inside the bag.

How to Play the Game:

Have the student choose a fish card and count and compare the sets of fish. Then, she should place the correct word card below each set to show which set has more and which has less. If the sets are equal, the student should place the "equal" card between the two sets. Play continues until all sets have been compared. The student should check her work by turning over each word card to see if the shape matches the one under the set of fish on the card.

Calendar Cats

Skill: Calendar Math

How to Make the Game:

1. Laminate and cut out the title piece, student instructions, calendar, day of the week cards, and number cards (pages B50–B53).
2. Attach the title piece and the student instructions to the front of a file folder.
3. Tape or glue the two sides of the calendar together and tape the entire calendar to the inside of the folder.
4. Place the game pieces in an envelope and attach it to the back of the folder with a paper clip.
5. Place copies of the "Look What I Learned" and the "On My Own" worksheets inside the folder.

How to Play the Game:

Have the student place the day of the week cards and number cards on the calendar in the correct order. The student should check his work by turning over each day of the week card and number card to see the matching shape from the blank on the calendar.

Day and Night

Skill: Time of Day

How to Make the Game:

1. Laminate and cut out the title piece, student instructions, game mats, and picture cards (pages B54–B58).
2. Attach the title piece and the student instructions to the front of a file folder.
3. Attach the day game mat to the left inside section of the folder and the night game mat to the right inside section of the folder.
4. Place the game pieces in an envelope and attach it to the back of the folder with a paper clip.
5. Place copies of the "Look What I Learned" and the "On My Own" worksheets inside the folder.

How to Play the Game:

Have the student choose a picture and decide if it shows a scene during the day or at night. She should then place the picture on the appropriate side of the folder. Play continues until each card has been placed on the correct game mat. The student should check her work by turning over each picture card to reveal a sun for day or a moon for night.

Spending Spree

Skill: Matching Sets of Coins to Money Values

How to Make the Game:

1. Laminate and cut out the title piece, student instructions, picture cards, and piggy banks (pages B59–B65).
2. Attach the title piece and the student instructions to the front of a large mailing envelope.
3. Place the picture cards, piggy banks, and copies of the "Look What I Learned" and the "On My Own" worksheets inside the envelope.

How to Play the Game:

Have the student choose a picture card and look at the price of the item. Then, he should match the picture card with the piggy bank that shows the correct amount of coins to buy the item. Play continues until each picture card has been matched with a piggy bank. The student should check his work by turning over each piggy bank to reveal the item that matches that amount of money.

Measuring Up

Skill: Nonstandard Measurement

How to Make the Game:

1. Laminate and cut out the title piece, student instructions, picture cards, number cards, and blocks strip (pages B66–B70).
2. Attach the title piece and the student instructions to the front of a large mailing envelope.
3. Place the picture cards, number cards, blocks strip, and copies of the "Look What I Learned" and the "On My Own" worksheets inside the envelope.

How to Play the Game:

Have the student choose a set of picture cards that are the same color. Then, she should use the strip of blocks to measure each object. She should find the number card with the correct measurement for the object and place it on the blank on the picture card. Then, the student should order the objects as "long," "longer," and "longest" on the game mat. The student should check her work by turning over each picture card to reveal the correct length and comparison word.

Candy Counting

Skill: Graphing

How to Make the Game:

1. Laminate and cut out the title piece, student instructions, candy jar, graph, and candy cards (pages B71–B74).
2. Attach the title piece and the student instructions to the front of a large mailing envelope.
3. Place the candy jar, graph, candy cards, and copies of the "Look What I Learned" and the "On My Own" worksheets inside the envelope.

How to Play the Game:

Have the student count one type of candy in the jar and place the matching number of candy cards on the graph to show how many pieces of that type of candy are in the jar. Play continues until each type of candy has been counted and graphed. The student should recreate the graph on the "Look What I Learned" worksheet by shading in one square in the correct column for each piece of candy.

Cookie Count

1. Place a number card in the box at the top of the cookie jar.

2. Count the correct number of cookies. Place them in the cookie jar.

3. Check your work. Turn over the number card to see the correct number of cookies.

4. Repeat for each number card.

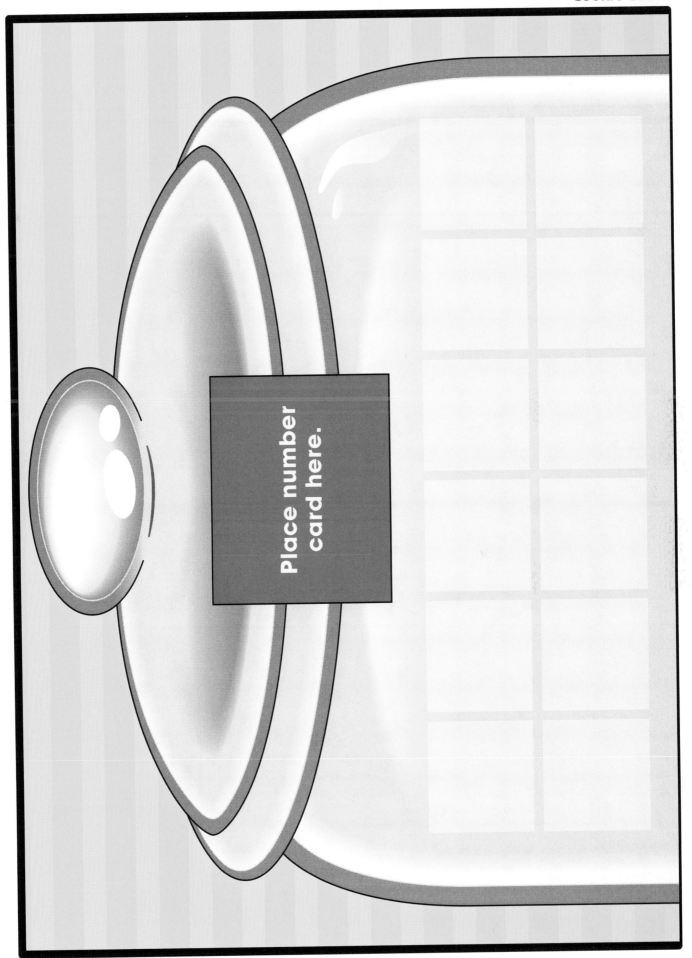

Place number card here.

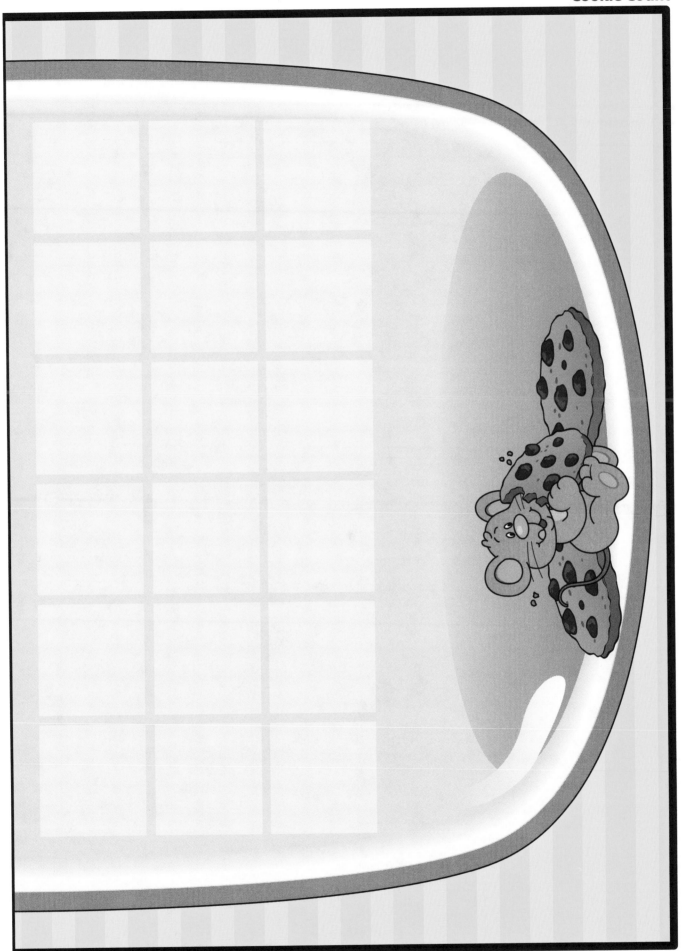

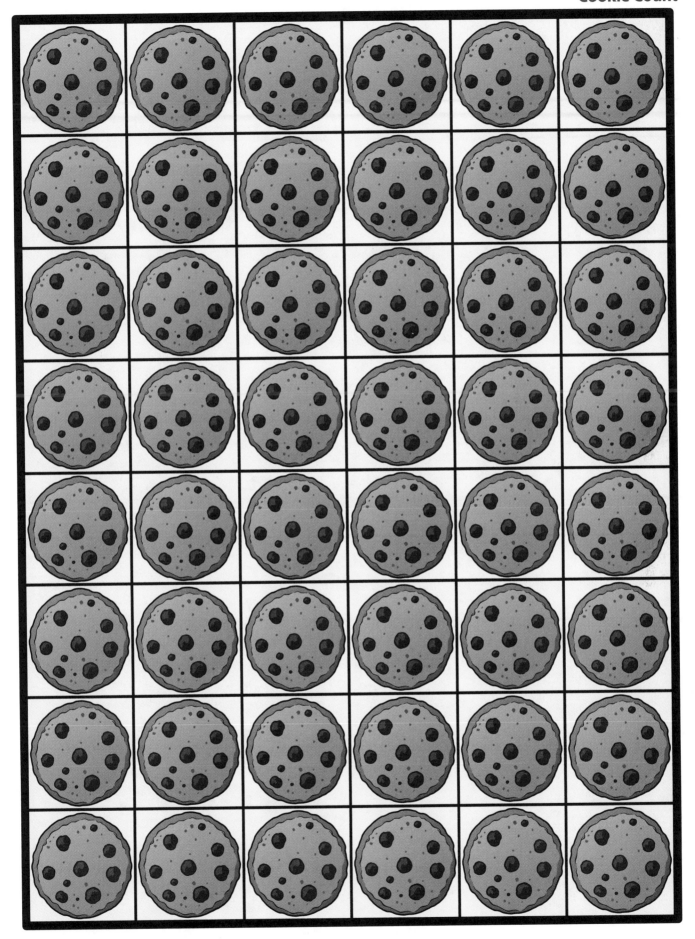

1	2	3
4	5	<u>6</u>
7	8	<u>9</u>
10	11	12
13	14	15

16	**17**	**18**
19	**20**	**21**
22	**23**	**24**
25	**26**	**27**
28	**29**	**30**

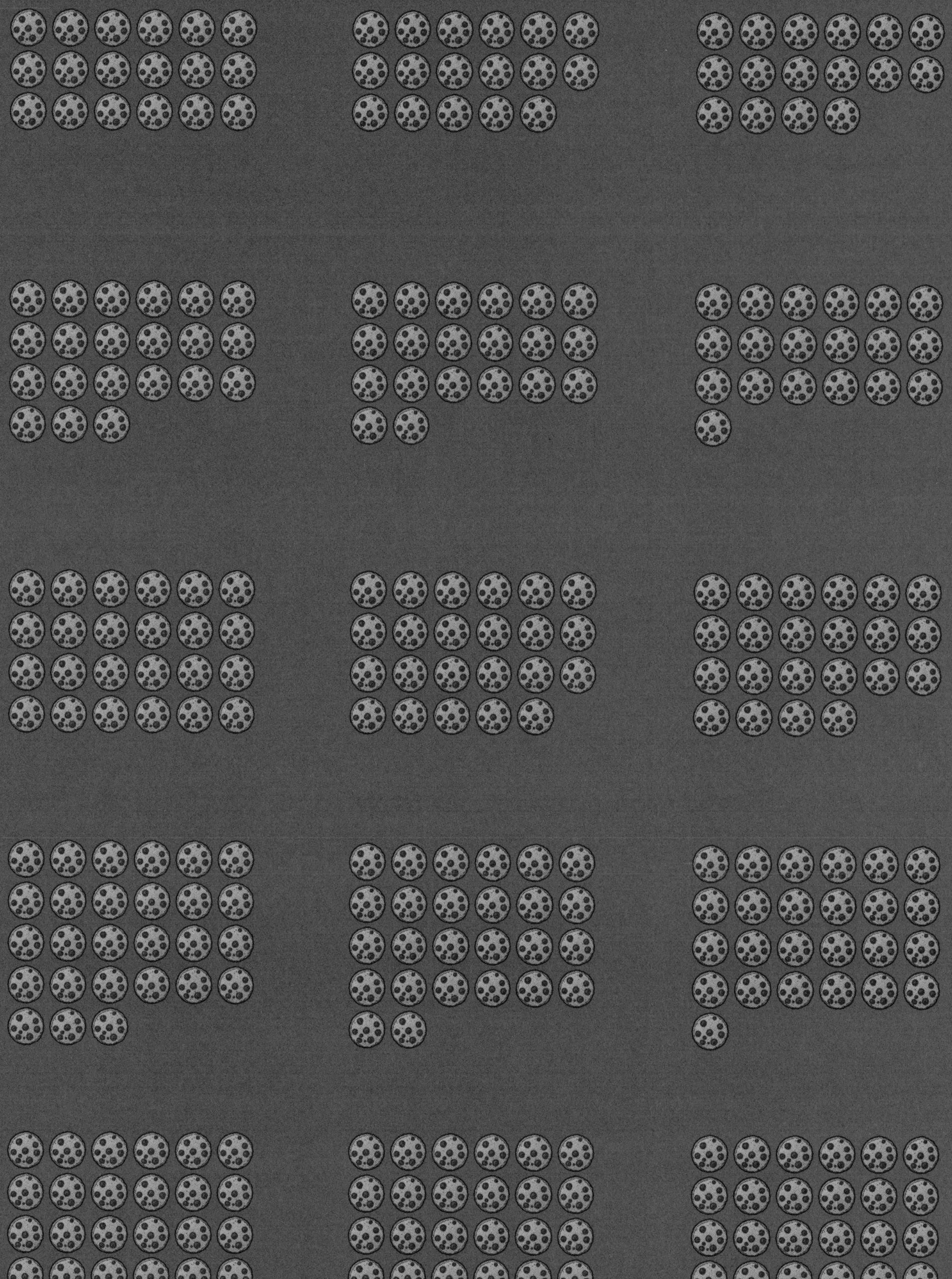

Up, Up, and Away

1. Look at the number word on a balloon.
2. Read the number word. Find the basket with the matching number.
3. Put the basket and balloon together. Repeat for each balloon.
4. Check your work. Turn over each basket to see the correct number word.

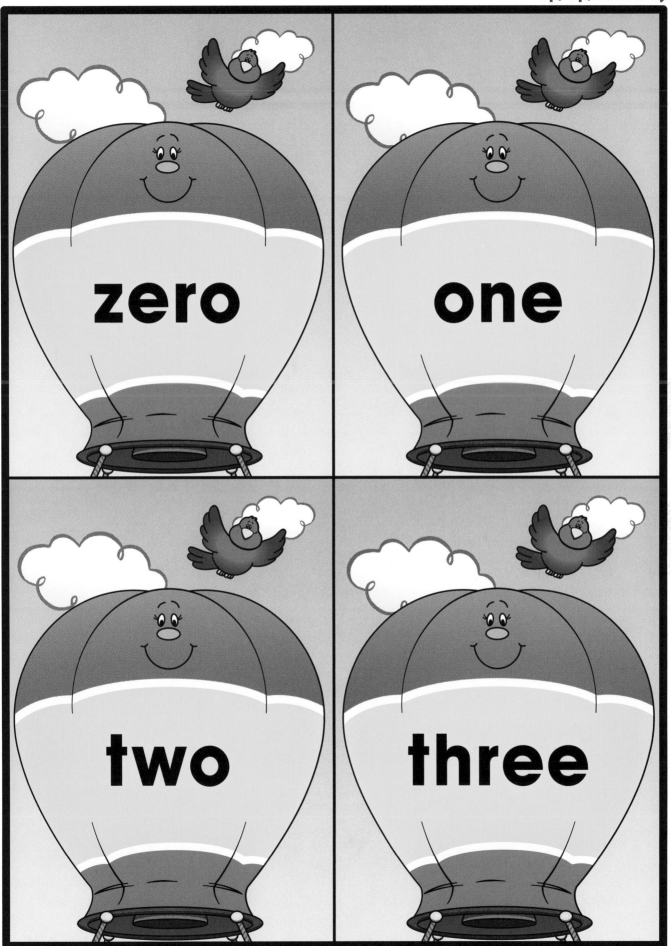

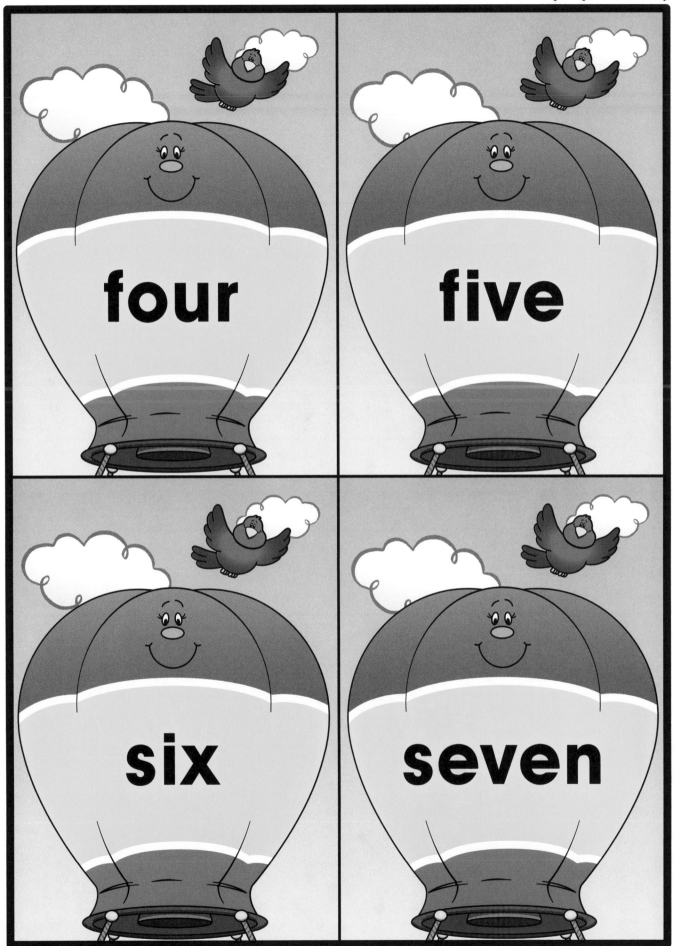

zero

two one

four three

six five

eight seven

ten nine

Count the Jelly Beans

1. Choose a jelly bean problem card. Count all of the jelly beans.
2. Find the jelly bean jar that shows the answer for the problem.
3. Find the number problem card that matches the complete jelly bean problem.
4. Check your work. Turn over the number problem card to see the correct jelly bean problem.

Count the Jelly Beans

$3 + 6 = 9$	$5 + 5 = 10$
$2 + 2 = 4$	$6 + 0 = 6$
$4 + 5 = 9$	$8 + 1 = 9$
$1 + 0 = 1$	$1 + 1 = 2$
$3 + 3 = 6$	$4 + 4 = 8$
$3 + 4 = 7$	$4 + 6 = 10$

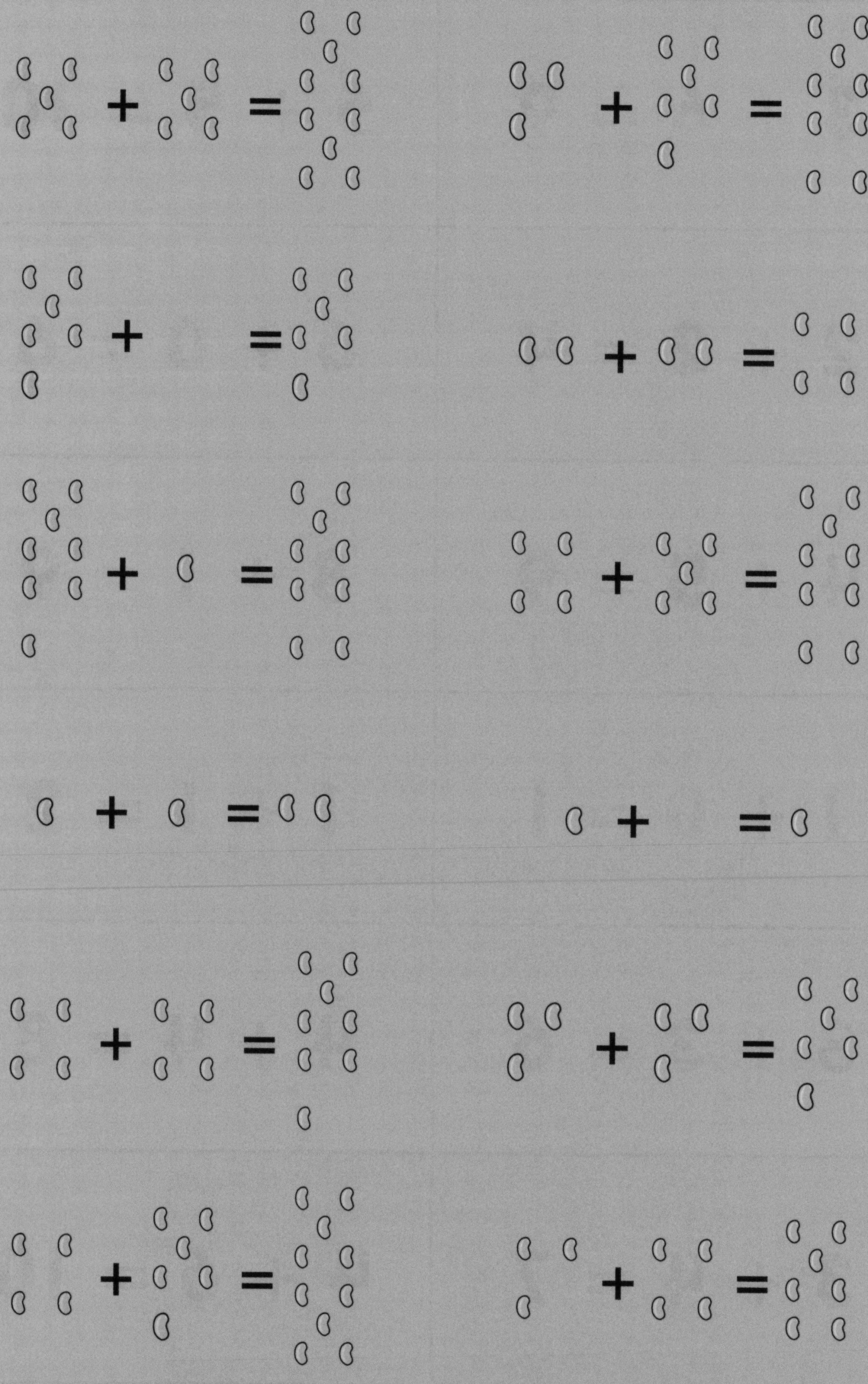

$0 + 4 = 4$

$1 + 5 = 6$

$4 + 1 = 5$

$3 + 2 = 5$

$1 + 2 = 3$

$5 + 2 = 7$

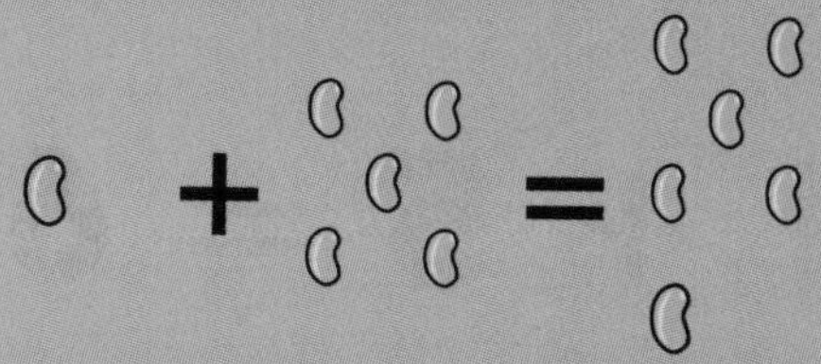

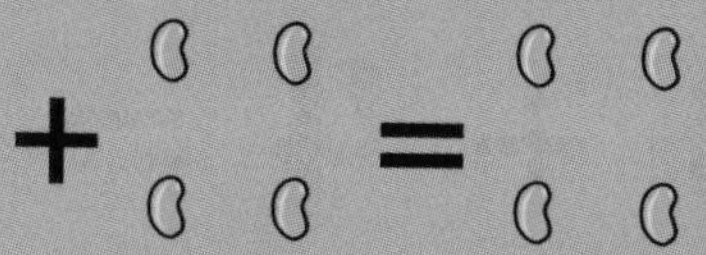

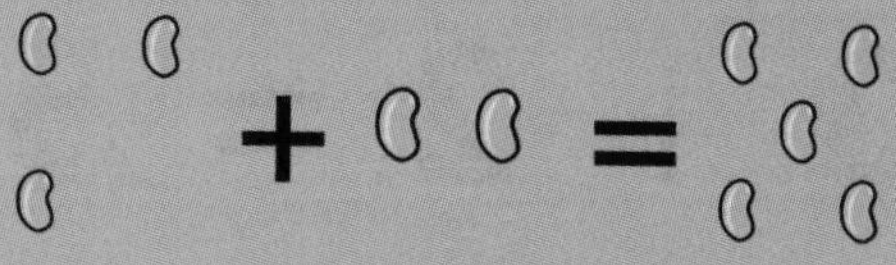

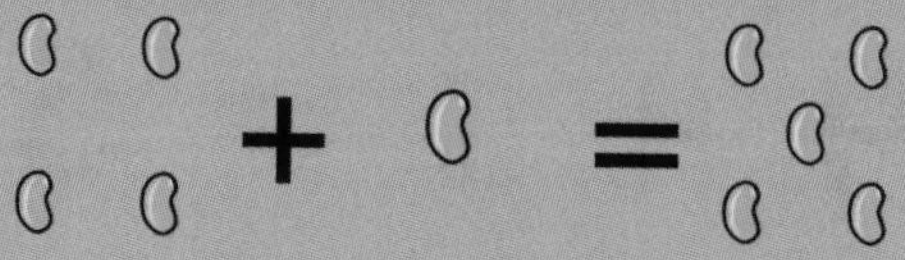

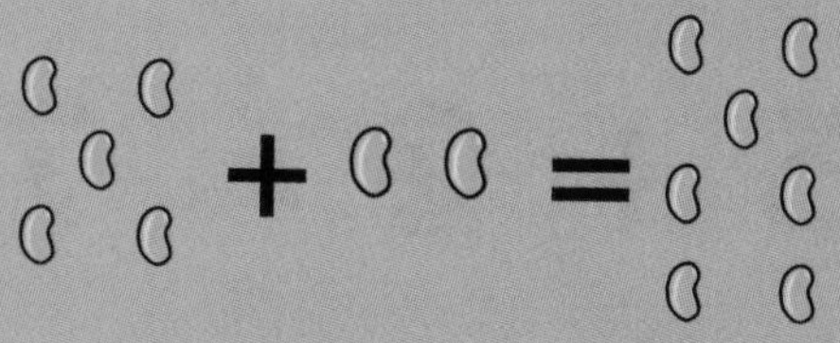

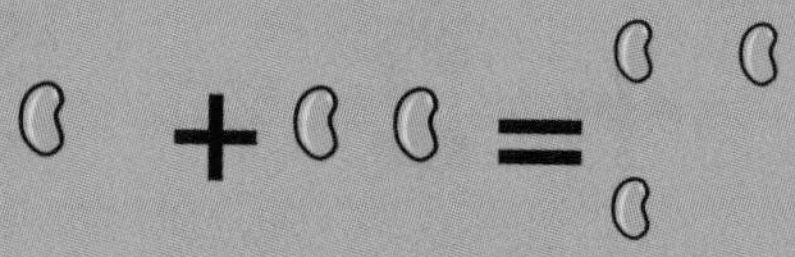

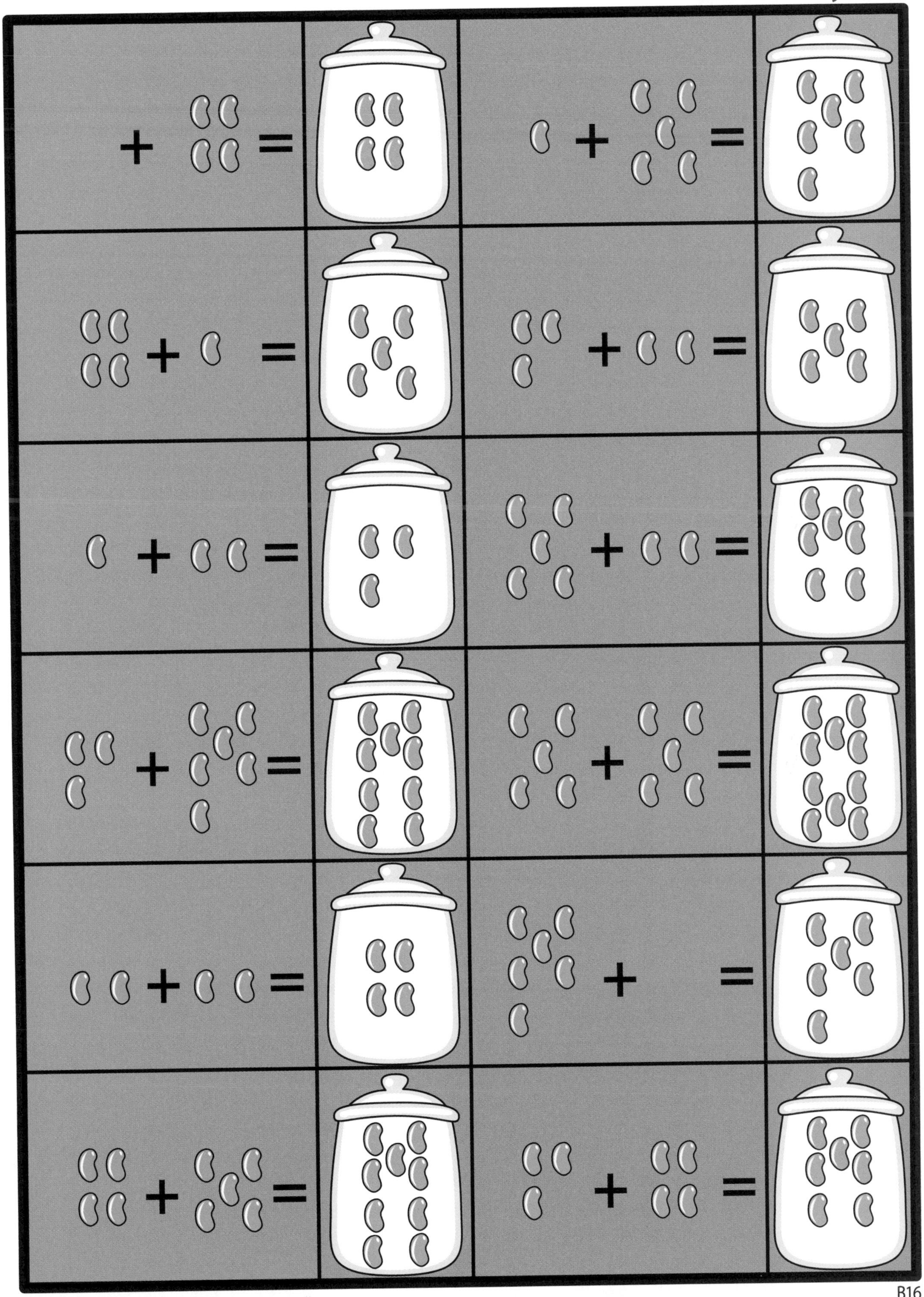

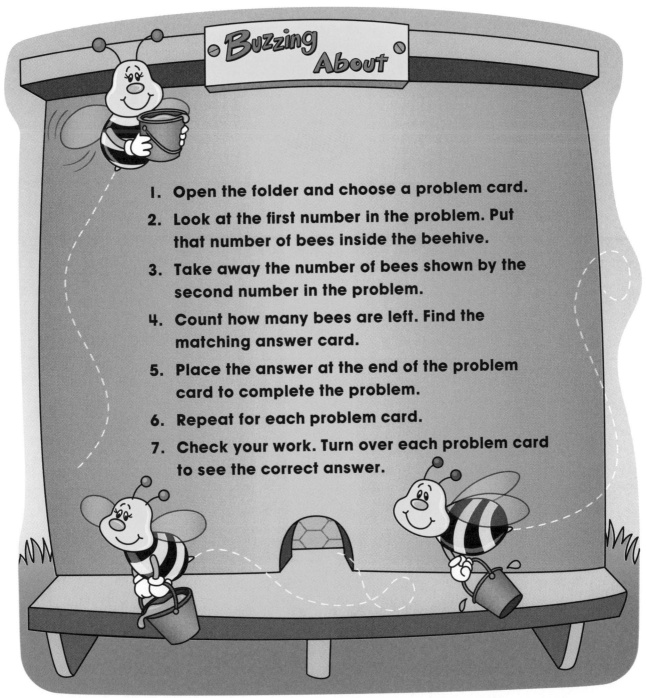

1. Open the folder and choose a problem card.
2. Look at the first number in the problem. Put that number of bees inside the beehive.
3. Take away the number of bees shown by the second number in the problem.
4. Count how many bees are left. Find the matching answer card.
5. Place the answer at the end of the problem card to complete the problem.
6. Repeat for each problem card.
7. Check your work. Turn over each problem card to see the correct answer.

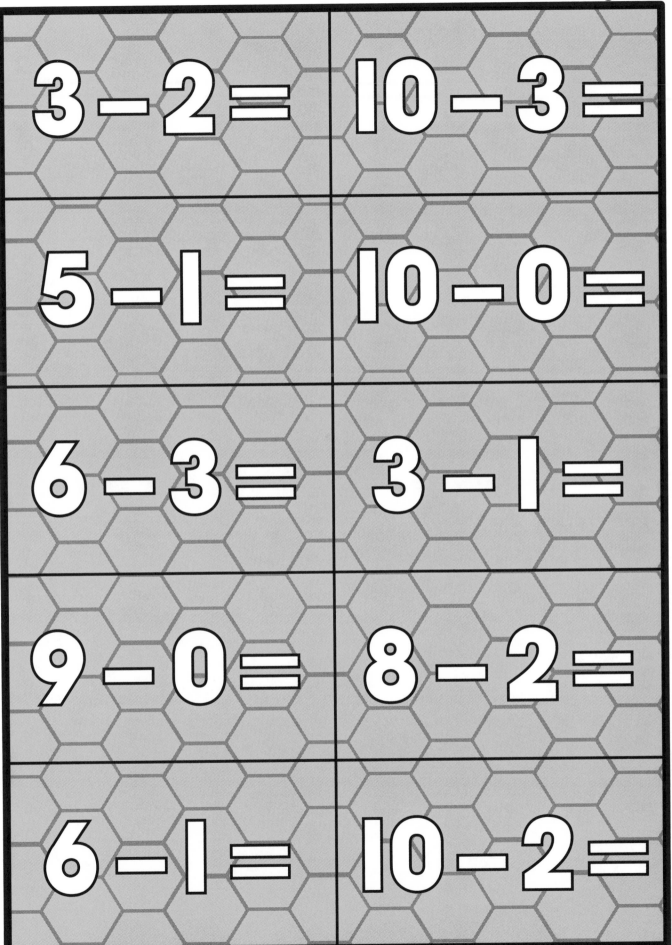

3 – 2 =

10 – 3 =

5 – 1 =

10 – 0 =

6 – 3 =

3 – 1 =

9 – 0 =

8 – 2 =

6 – 1 =

10 – 2 =

7	1
10	4
2	3
<u>6</u>	<u>9</u>
8	5

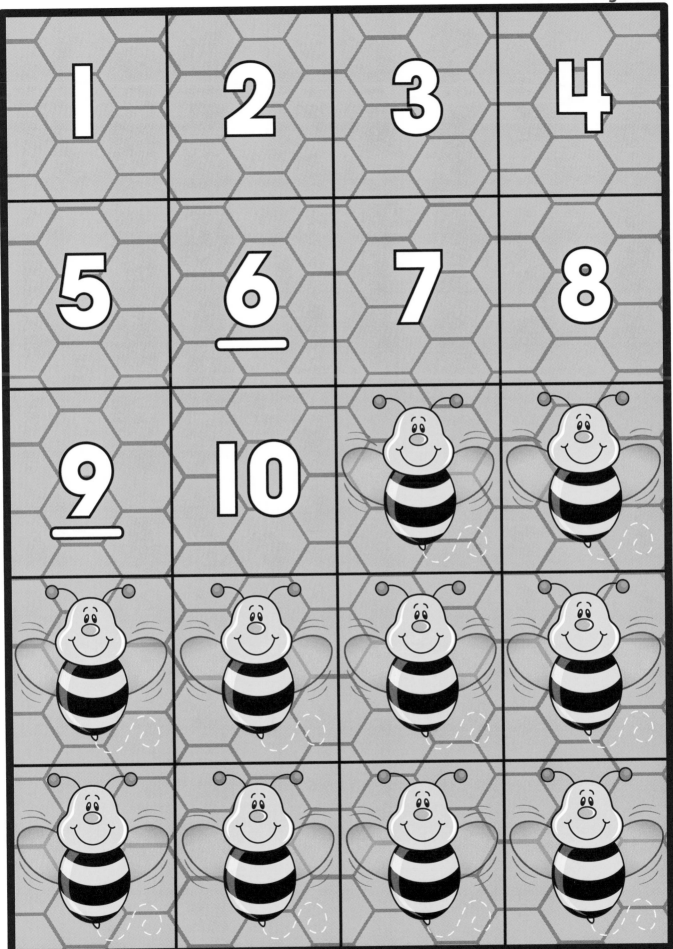

Doggone Fun!

1. Lay out the dog picture cards and bones.
2. Choose a picture card.
3. Find the bone with the word that tells about each picture on the card.
4. Put the correct word with each picture.
5. Repeat for each picture card.
6. Check your work. Turn over each picture card to see the correct words.

outside

inside

under

over

down

up

on

between

beside

behind

in front of

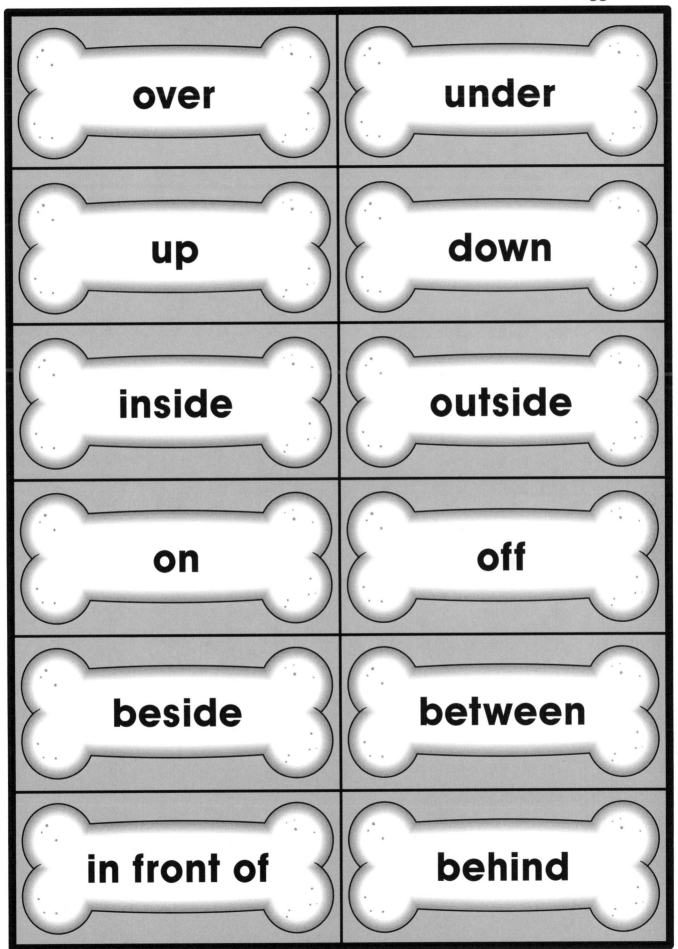

over

under

up

down

inside

outside

on

off

beside

between

in front of

behind

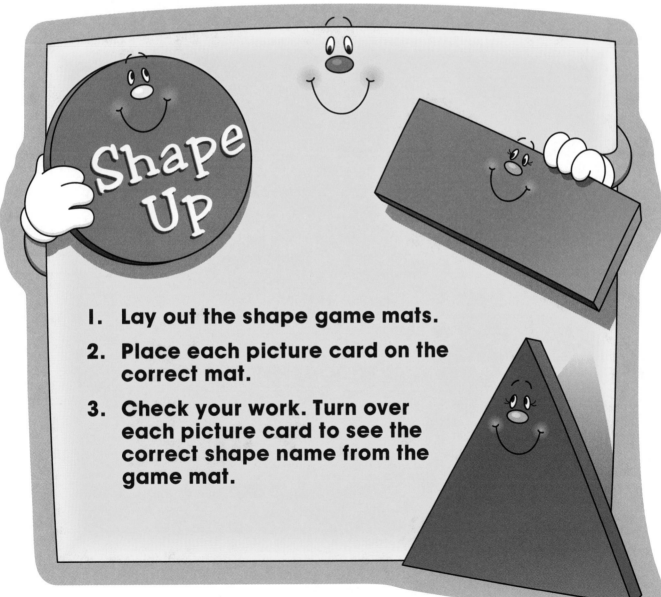

1. Lay out the shape game mats.

2. Place each picture card on the correct mat.

3. Check your work. Turn over each picture card to see the correct shape name from the game mat.

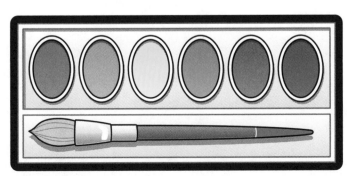

Circle

Rectangle

Rectangle

Circle

Circle

Circle

Rectangle

Rectangle

Triangle

Triangle

Triangle

Triangle

Square

Square

Square

Square

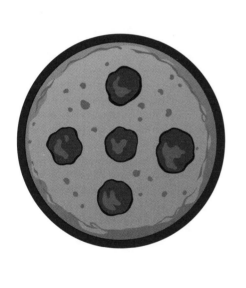

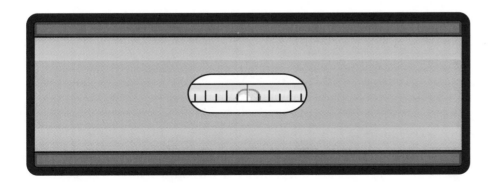

Square   Square

                    Circle   Circle

Rectangle

                              Rectangle

Rectangle

Square

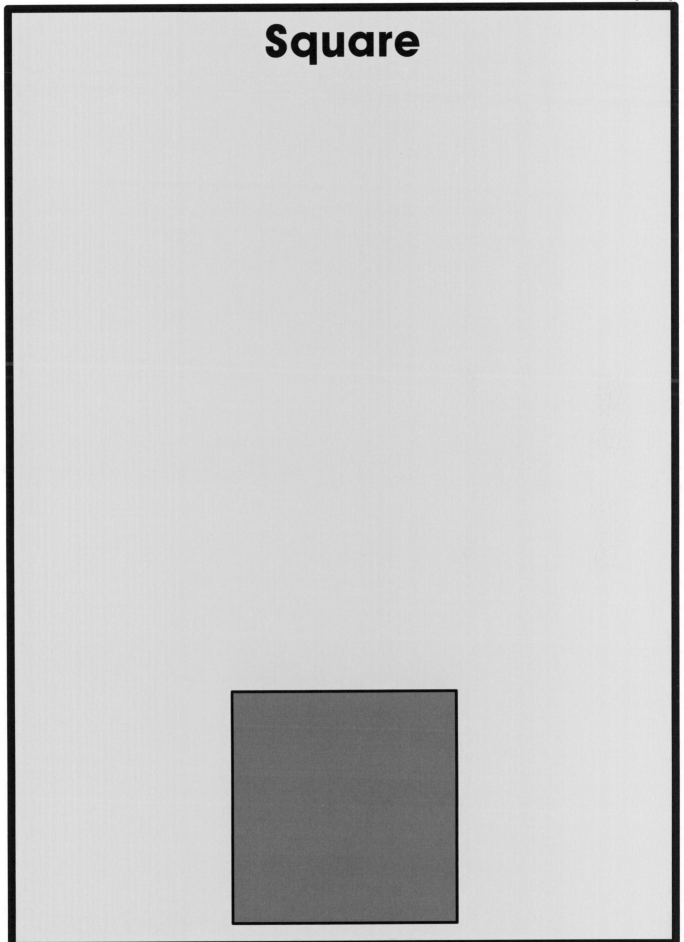

Triangle

Circle

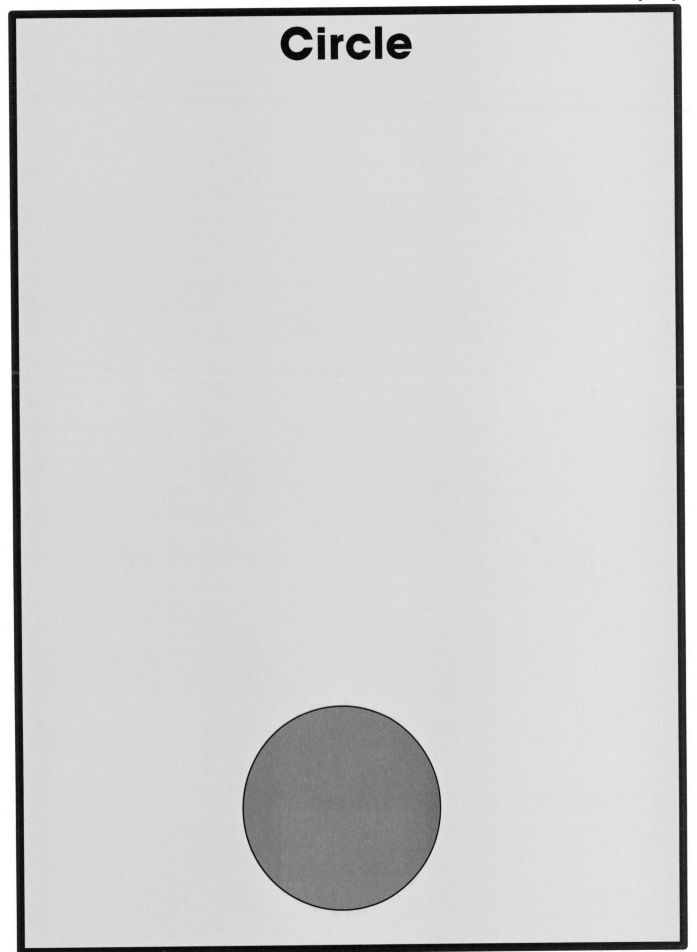

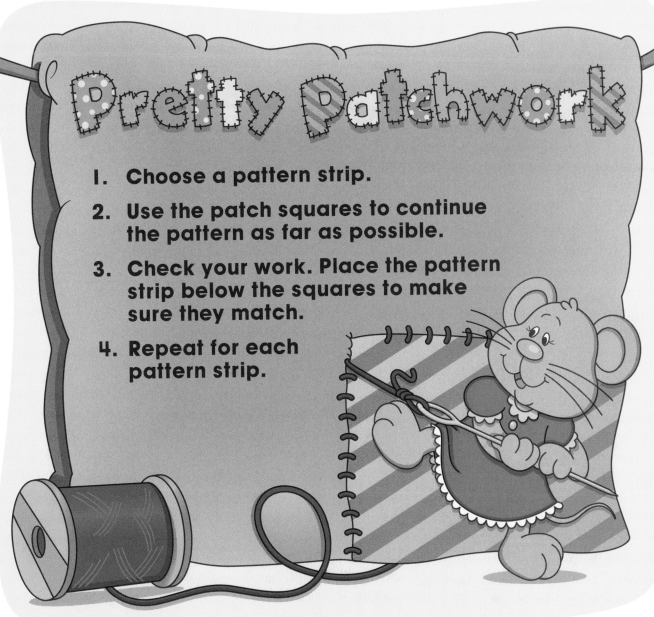

Pretty Patchwork

1. Choose a pattern strip.

2. Use the patch squares to continue the pattern as far as possible.

3. Check your work. Place the pattern strip below the squares to make sure they match.

4. Repeat for each pattern strip.

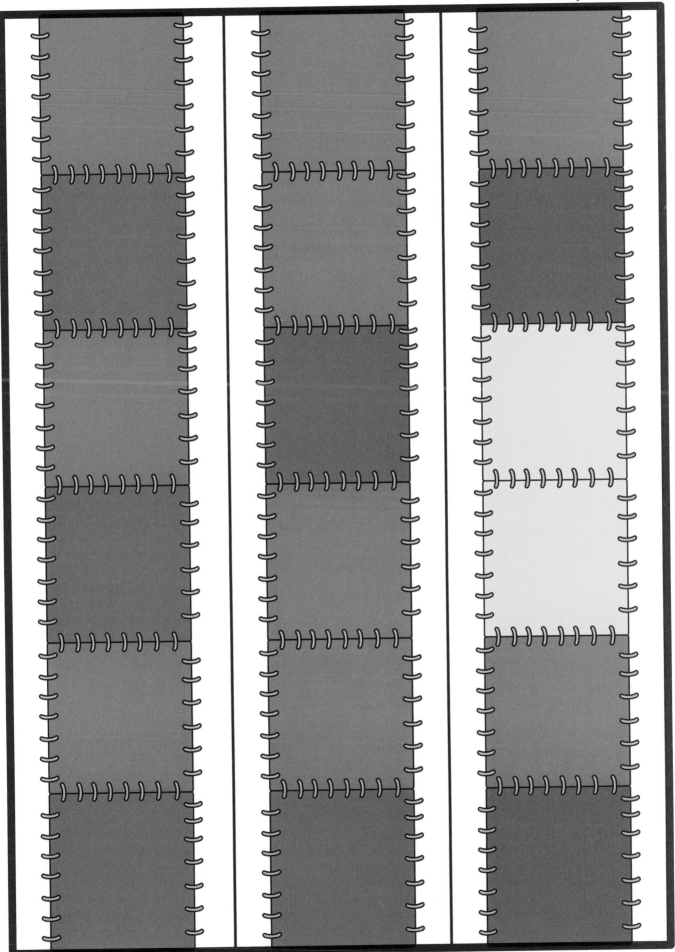

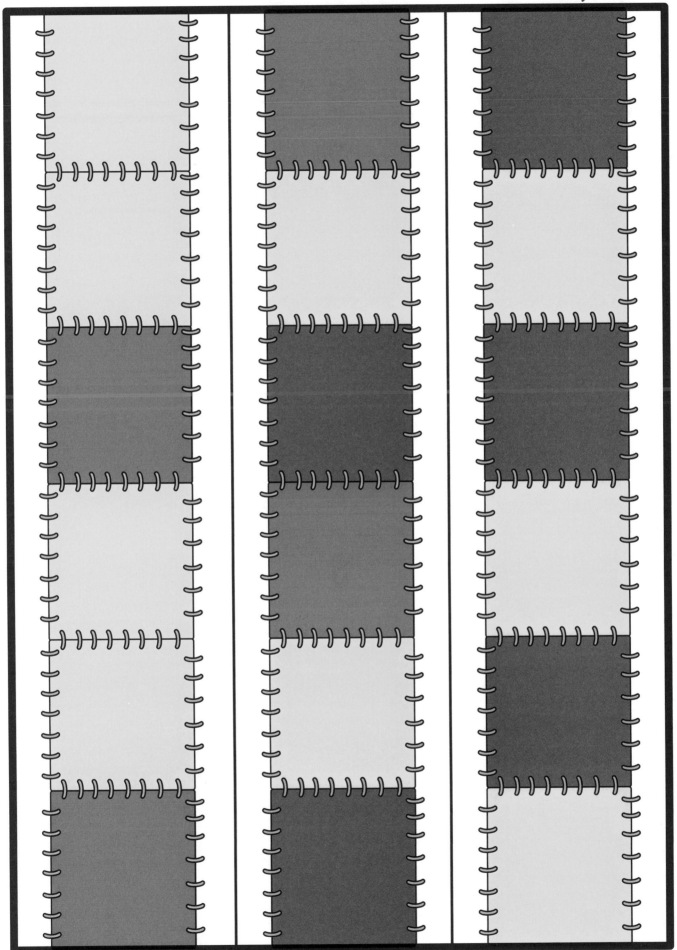

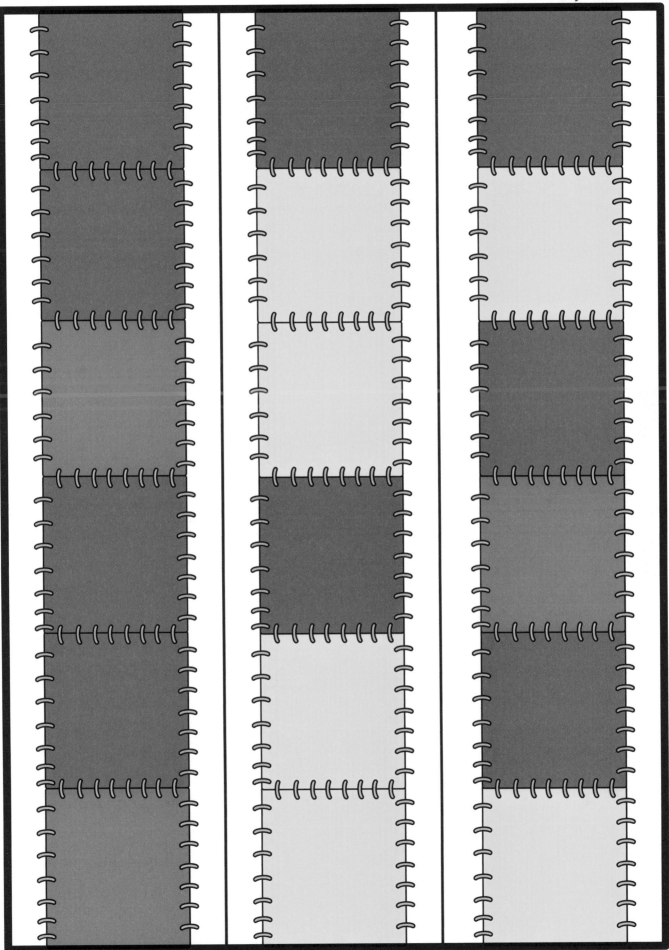

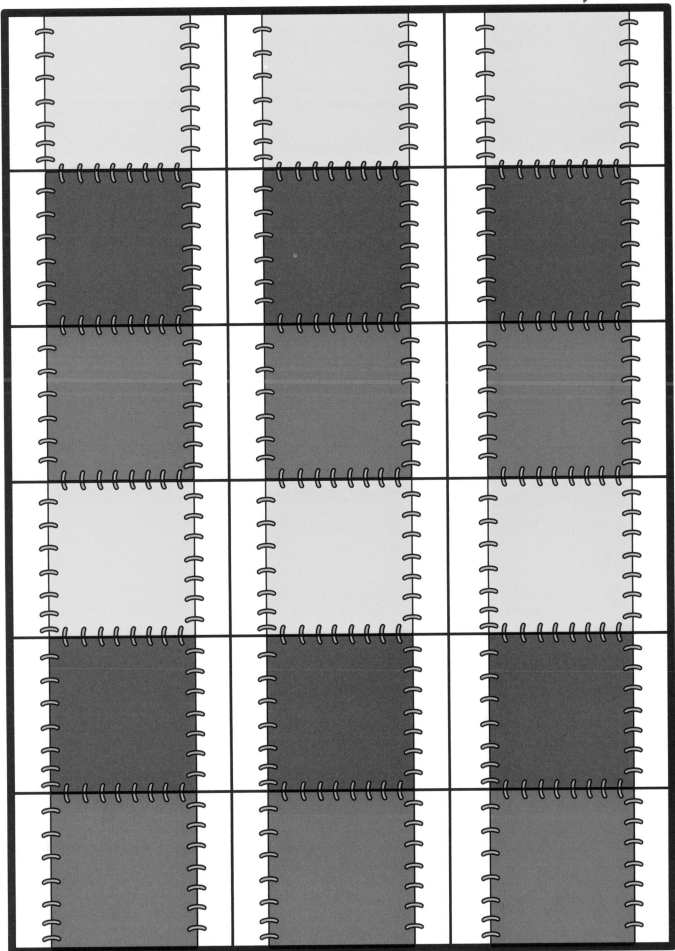

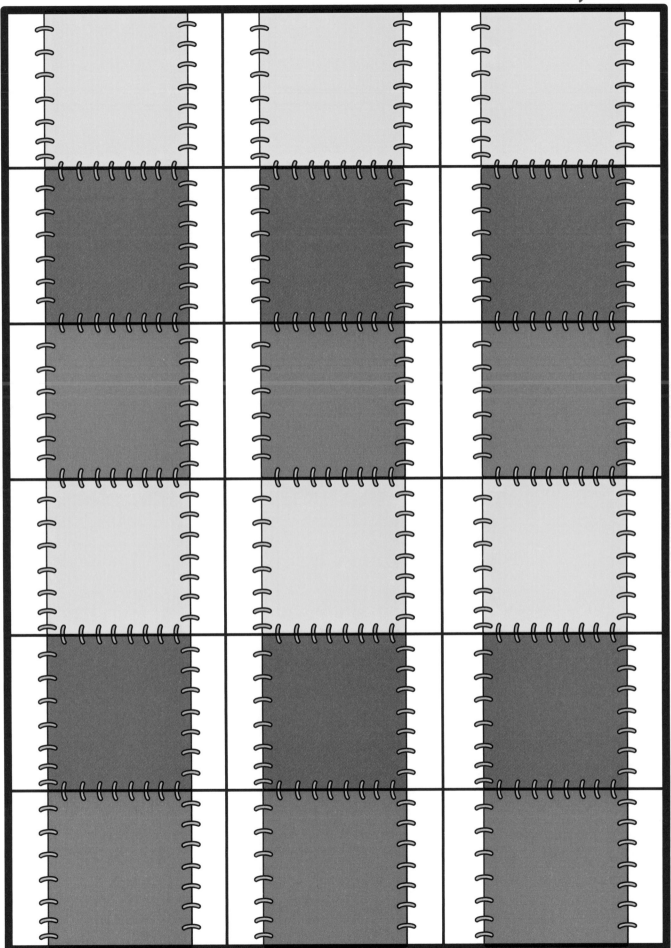

1. Put the vases in order from 1 to 10.

2. Choose a flower card. Count the flowers.

3. Match the flower card to the vase card with the correct number.

4. Repeat for each flower card.

5. Check your work. Turn over each flower card to see the number from the correct vase.

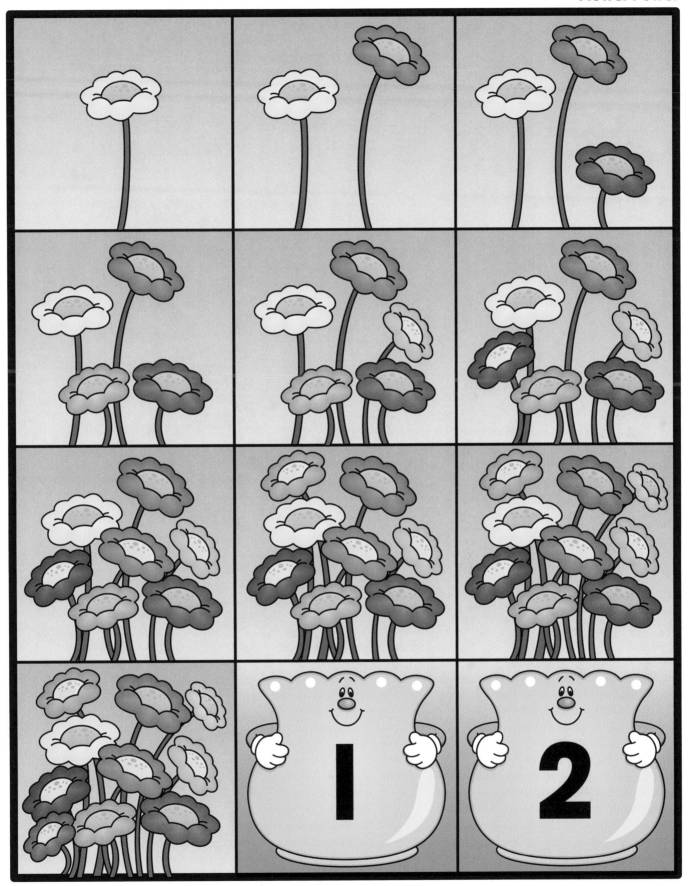

3

2

1

6

5

4

9

8

7

10

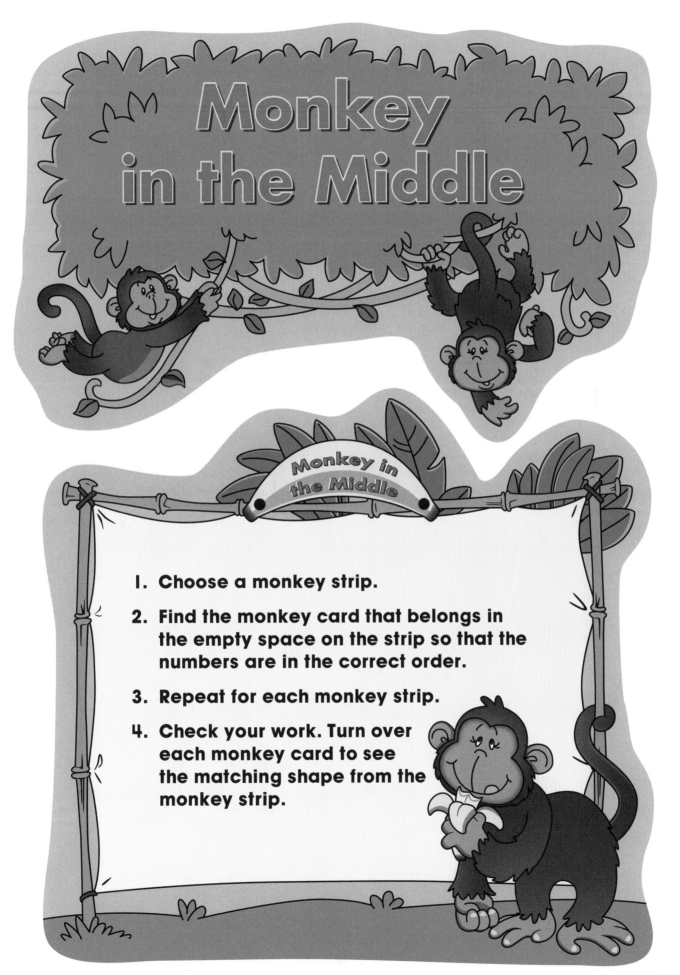

Monkey in the Middle

Monkey in the Middle

1. Choose a monkey strip.

2. Find the monkey card that belongs in the empty space on the strip so that the numbers are in the correct order.

3. Repeat for each monkey strip.

4. Check your work. Turn over each monkey card to see the matching shape from the monkey strip.

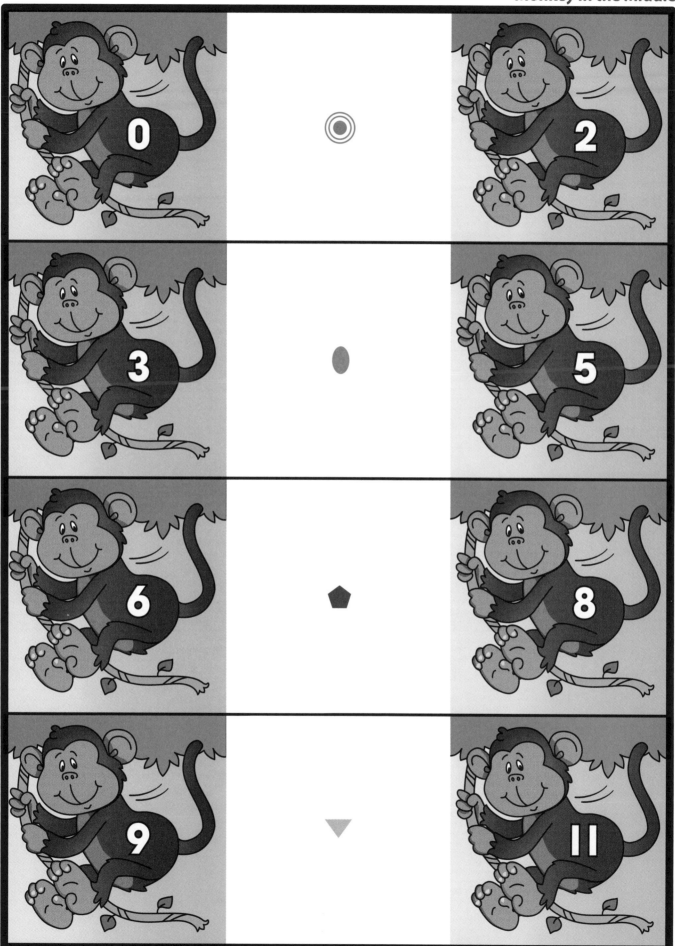

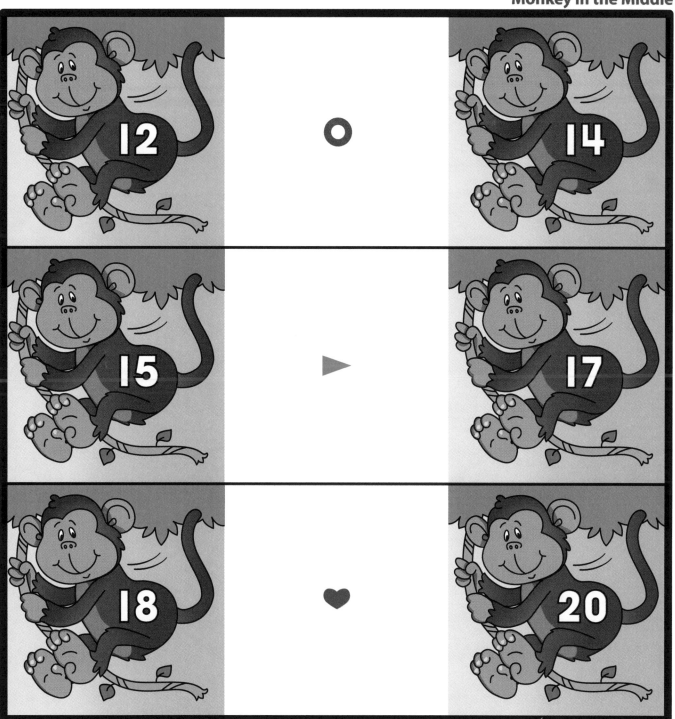

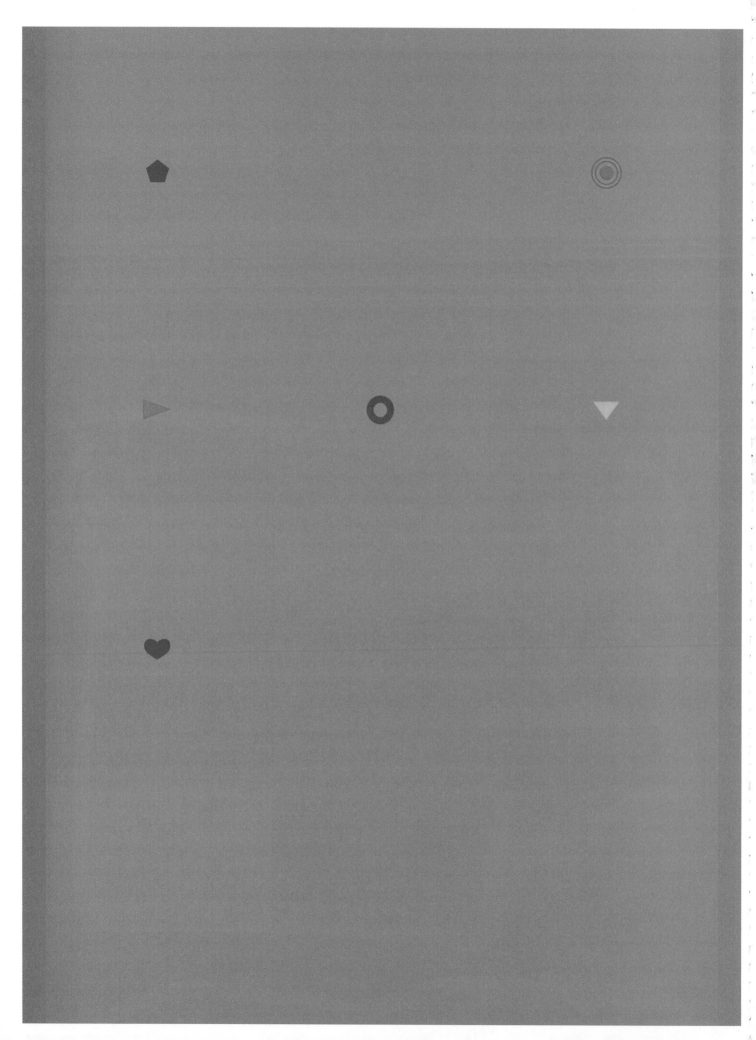

Gone Fishing

1. Choose a fish picture card.

2. Count the fish in each set.

3. Place a word card below each set to show which set has more and which has less. If the sets are equal, place the "equal" card between the two sets.

4. Repeat for each fish card.

5. Check your work. Turn over each word card to see the matching shape from the fish card.

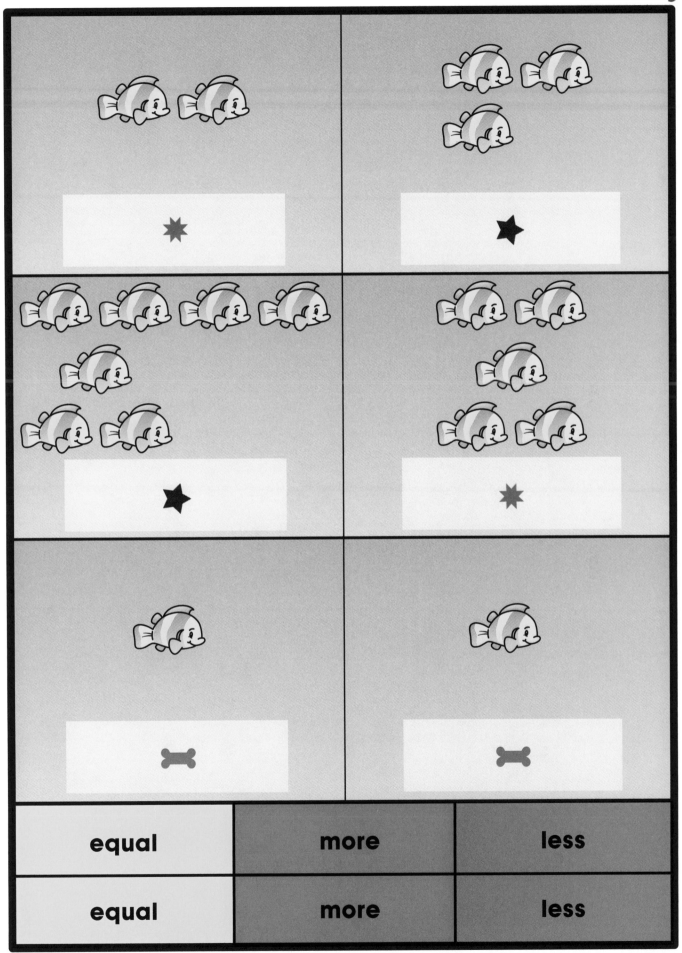

equal	more	less
equal	more	less

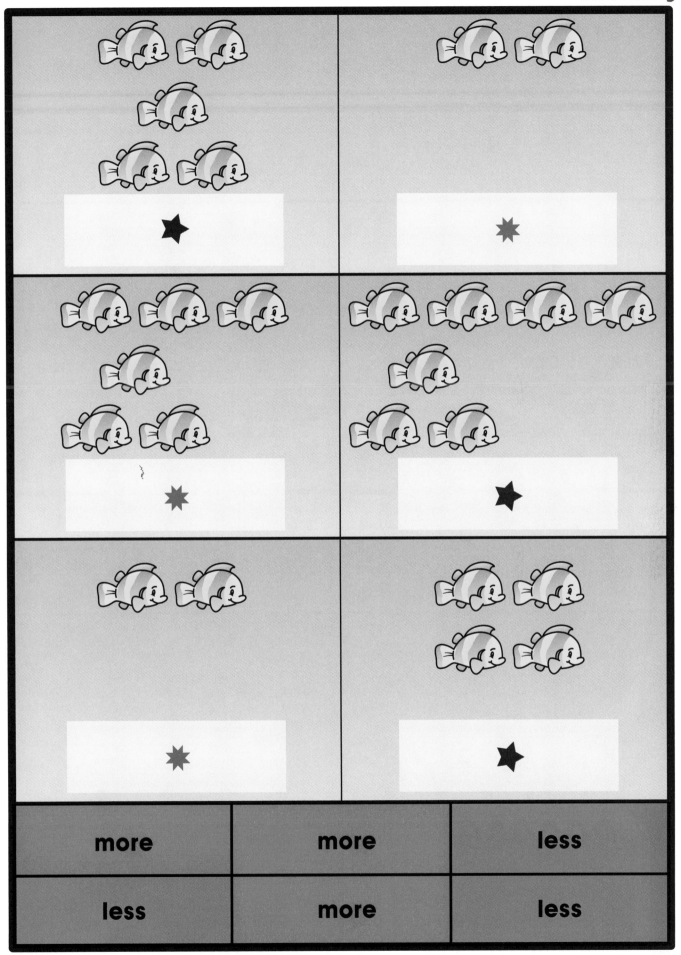

| more | more | less |
| less | more | less |

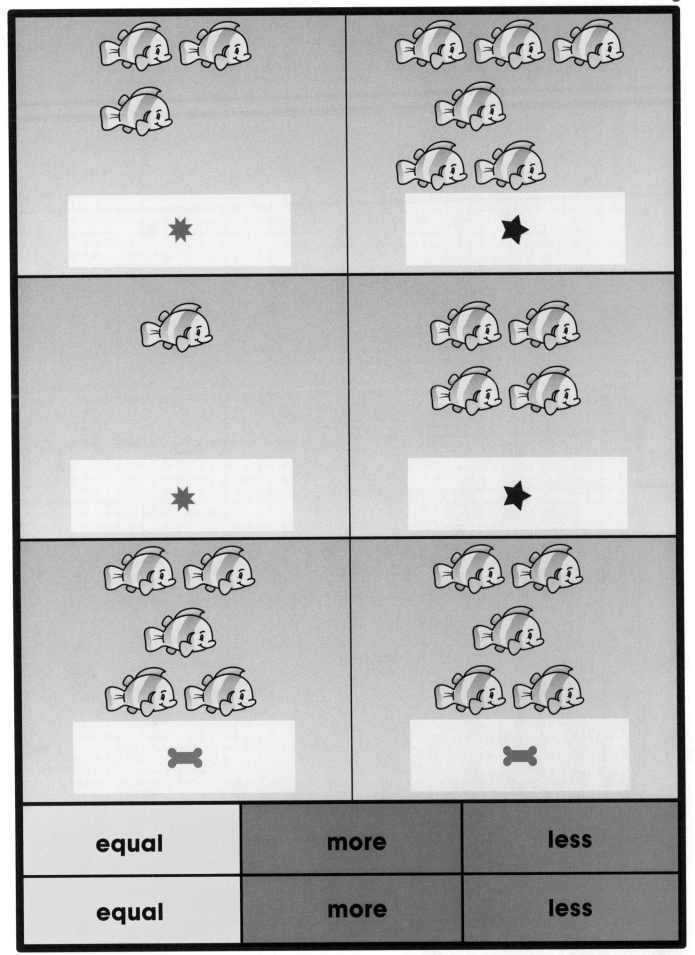

equal	more	less
equal	more	less

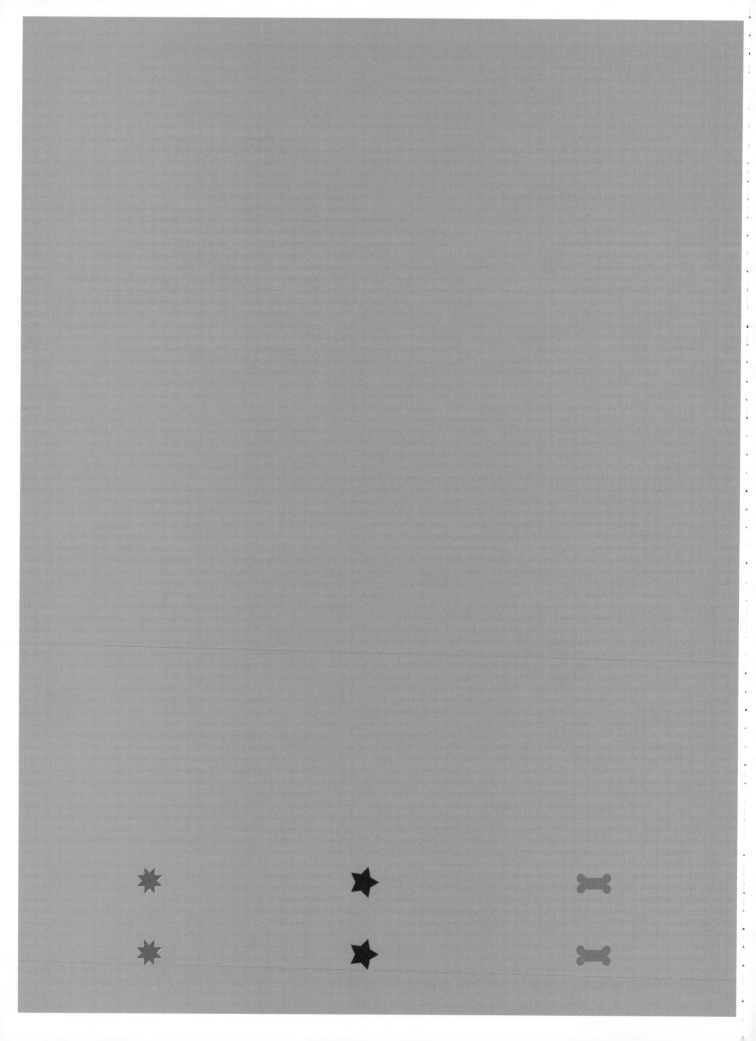

Calendar Cats

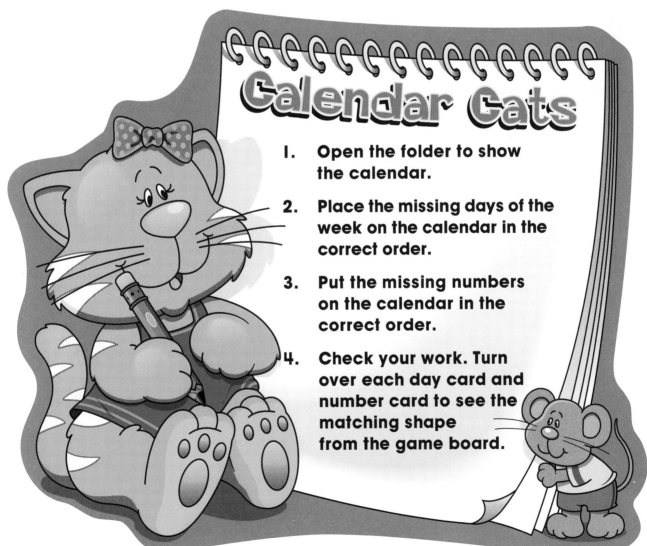

Calendar Cats

1. Open the folder to show the calendar.

2. Place the missing days of the week on the calendar in the correct order.

3. Put the missing numbers on the calendar in the correct order.

4. Check your work. Turn over each day card and number card to see the matching shape from the game board.

Sunday	✖	▰
1	2	3
★	9	10
15	16	♥
22	◼	24
29	✴	31

◎	●	▼	**Saturday**
4	●	6	7
○	12	13	🌙
▶	19	20	21
25	⬟	27	⬠

5	**8**	**11**	**14**
17	**18**	**23**	**26**
28	**30**	Monday	Tuesday
Wednesday	Thursday	Friday	

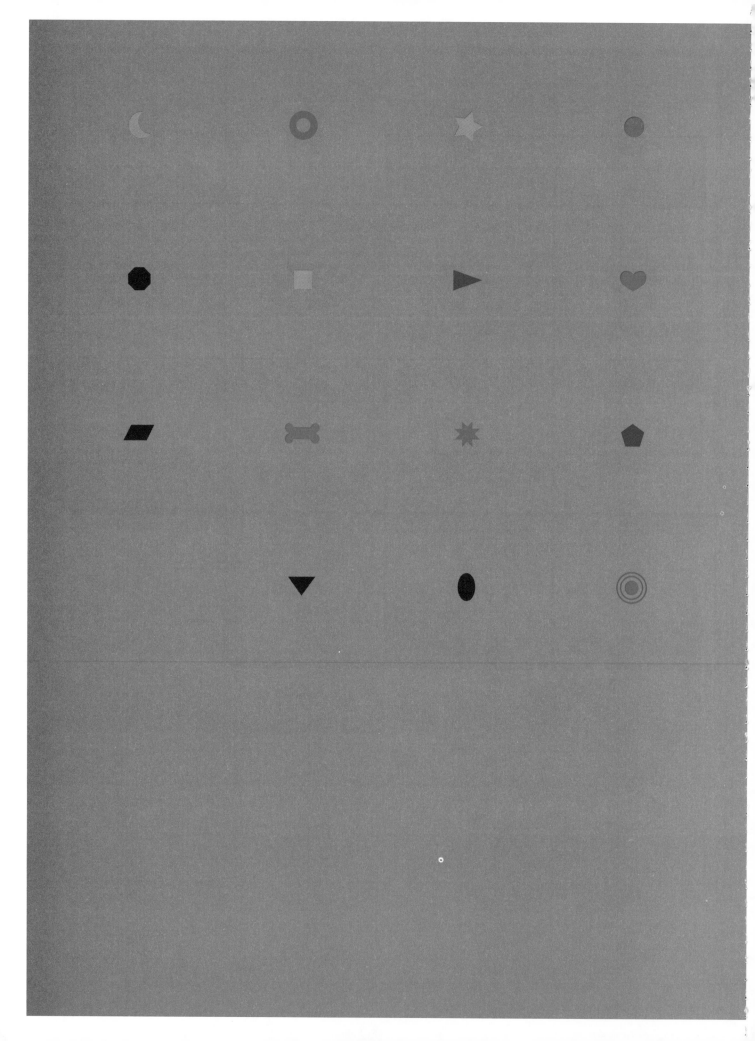

Day and Night

1. Open the folder and stack the cards picture-side up.

2. Choose a picture card.

3. Place the picture on the correct side of the folder to show whether the scene happens at night or during the day.

4. Check your work. Turn over each picture card to see a moon for night or a sun for day.

1. Choose a picture card. Find the piggy bank with the correct number of coins to buy the item.
2. Match the picture card with the piggy bank.
3. Repeat for each picture card.
4. Check your work. Turn over each piggy bank to see the correct item for that amount of money.

80¢

63¢

20¢

10¢

42¢

6¢

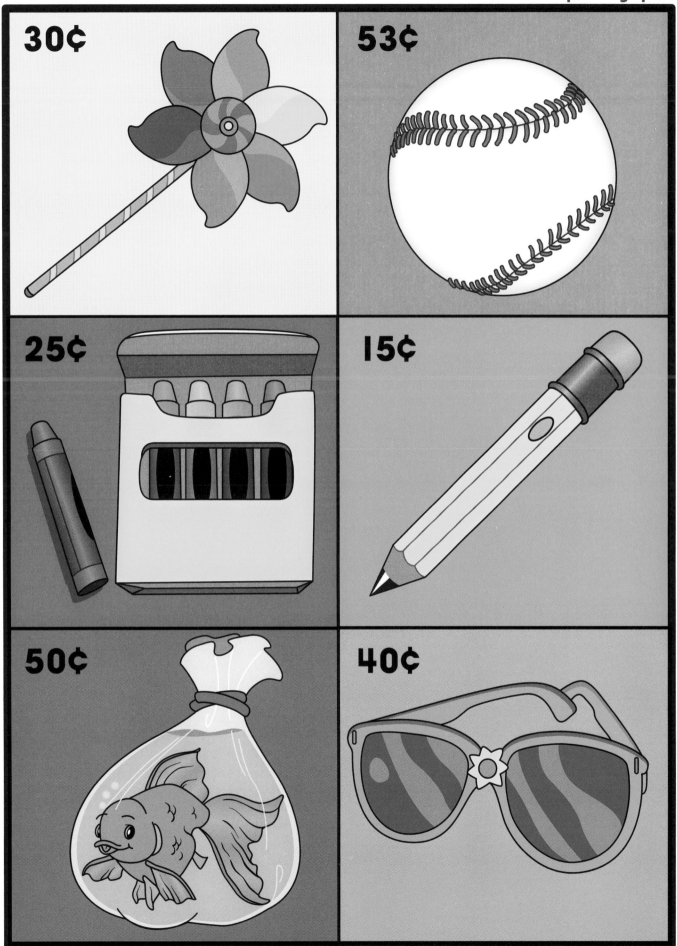

72¢

22¢

34¢

16¢

43¢

70¢

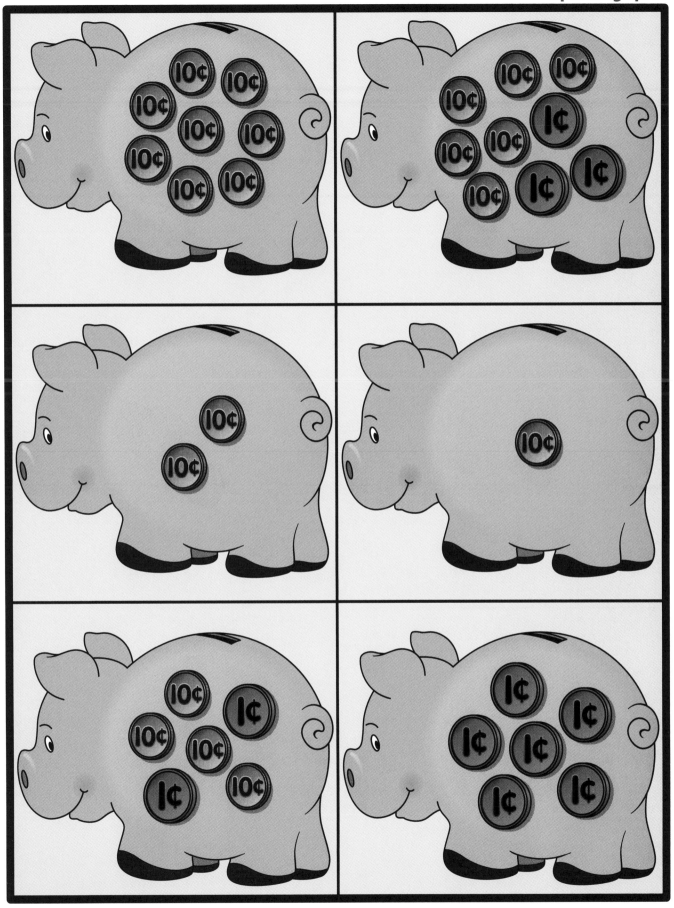

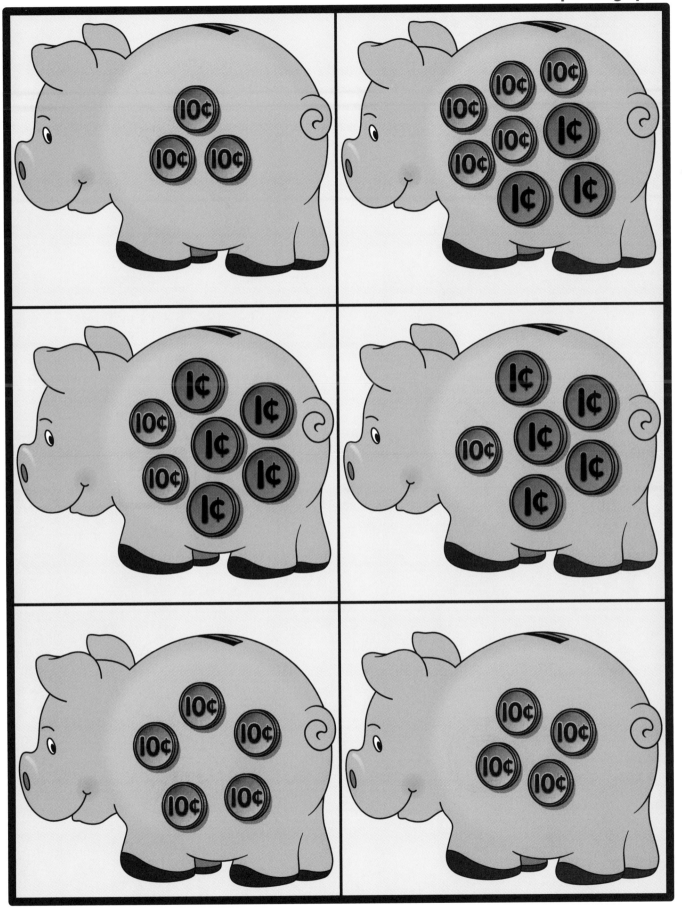

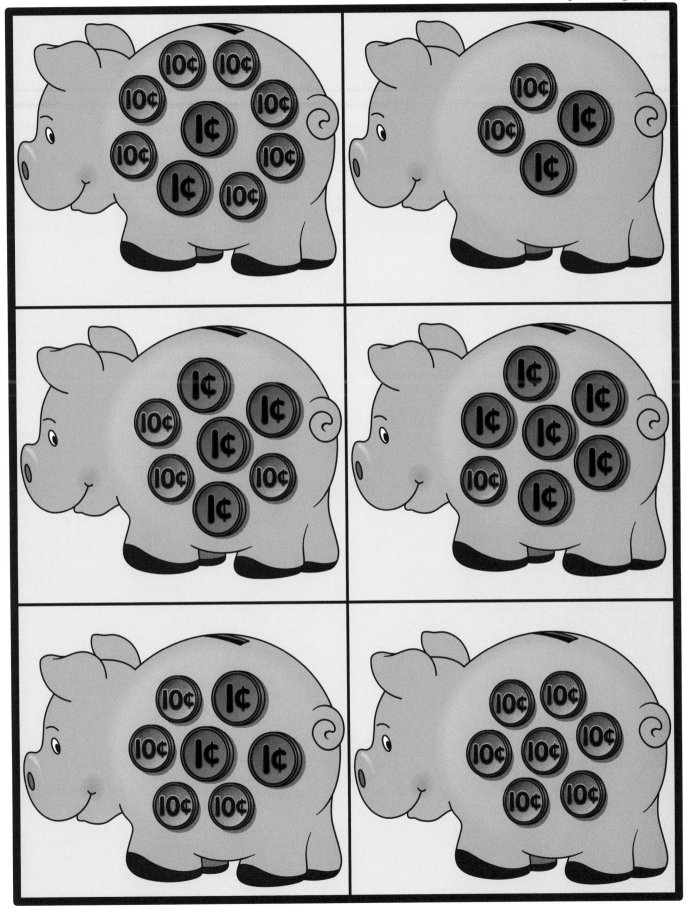

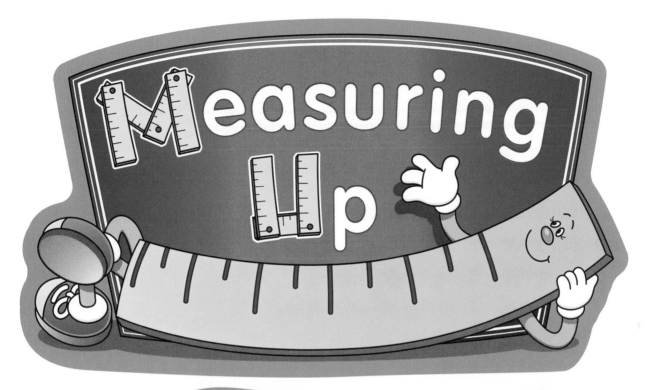

Measuring Up

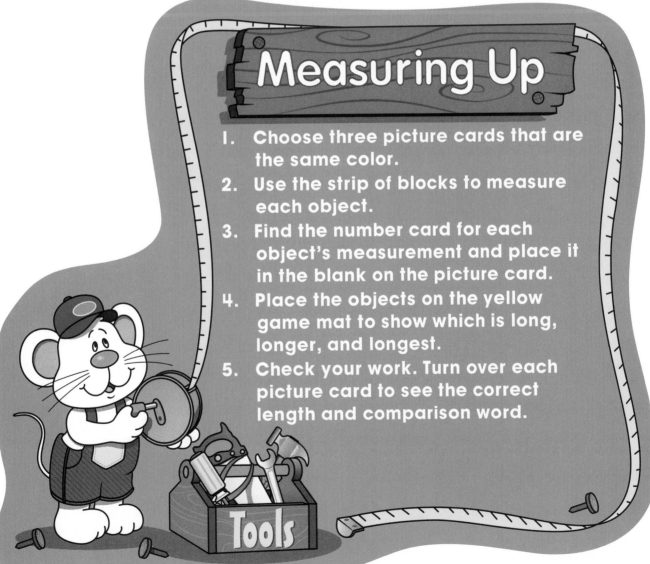

1. Choose three picture cards that are the same color.
2. Use the strip of blocks to measure each object.
3. Find the number card for each object's measurement and place it in the blank on the picture card.
4. Place the objects on the yellow game mat to show which is long, longer, and longest.
5. Check your work. Turn over each picture card to see the correct length and comparison word.

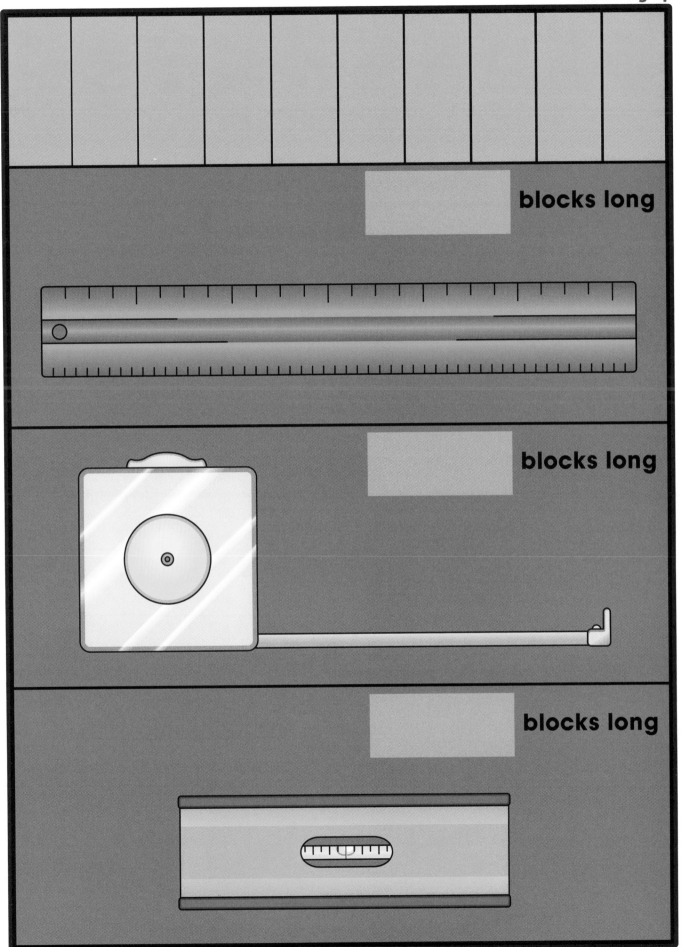

blocks long

blocks long

blocks long

Longest
9 blocks long

Longer
8 blocks long

Long
5 blocks long

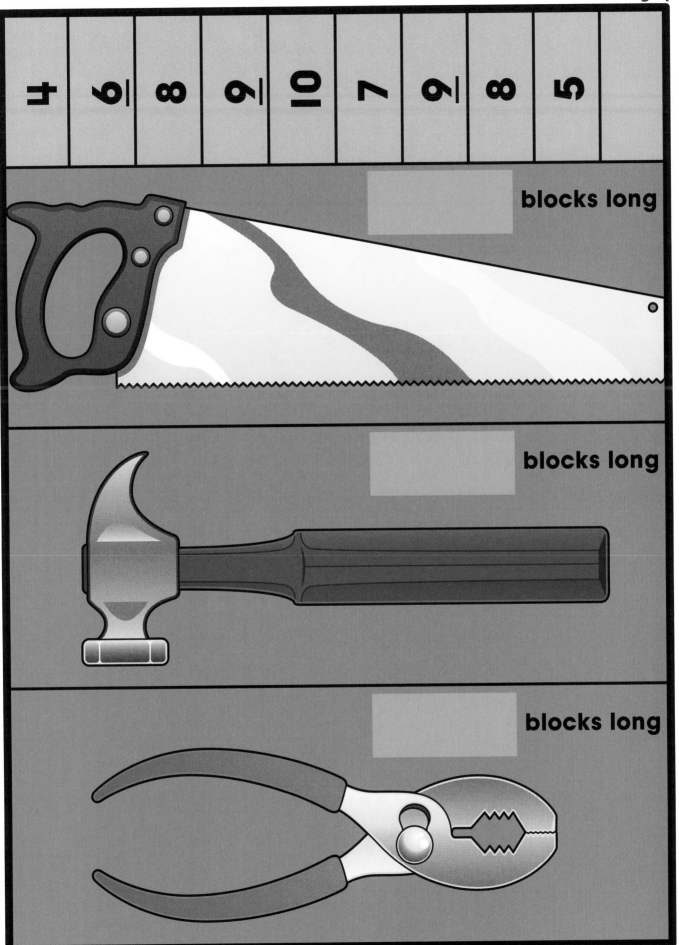

4   6   8   9   10   7   9   8   5

blocks long

blocks long

blocks long

**Longest
10 blocks long**

**Longer
8 blocks long**

**Long
7 blocks long**

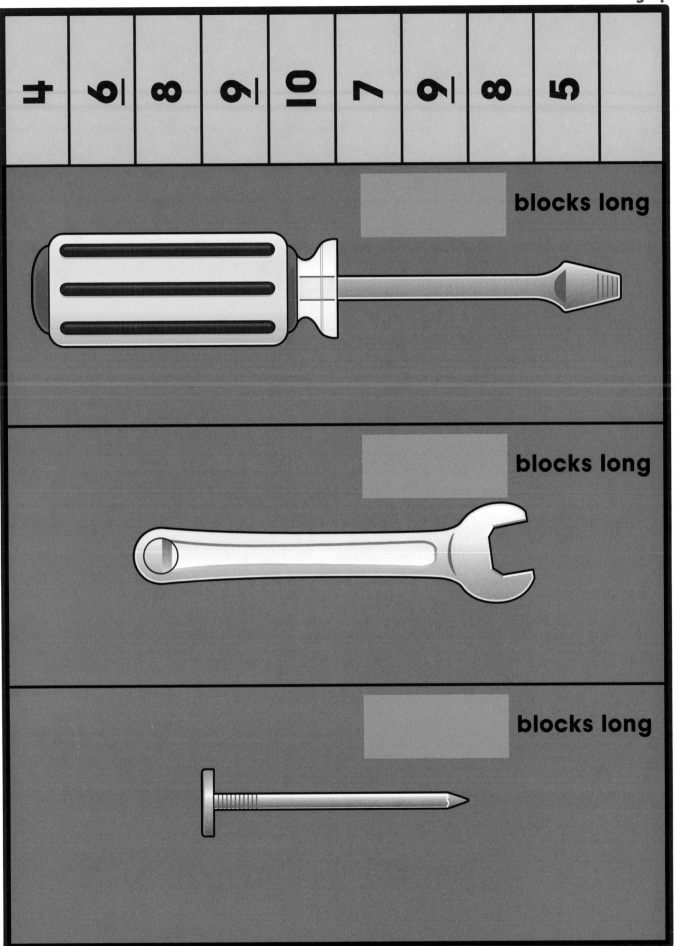

4 6 8 9 10 7 9 8 5

blocks long

blocks long

blocks long

Longest
9 blocks long

Longer
6 blocks long

Long
4 blocks long

Long

Longer

Longest

Candy Counting

Candy Counting

1. Choose a type of candy. Count the number of that candy in the candy jar.
2. Place a picture of the candy on the graph for each piece of candy in the jar.
3. Repeat for each type of candy.
4. For each piece of candy, color a space on the graph on the "Look What I Learned" worksheet.

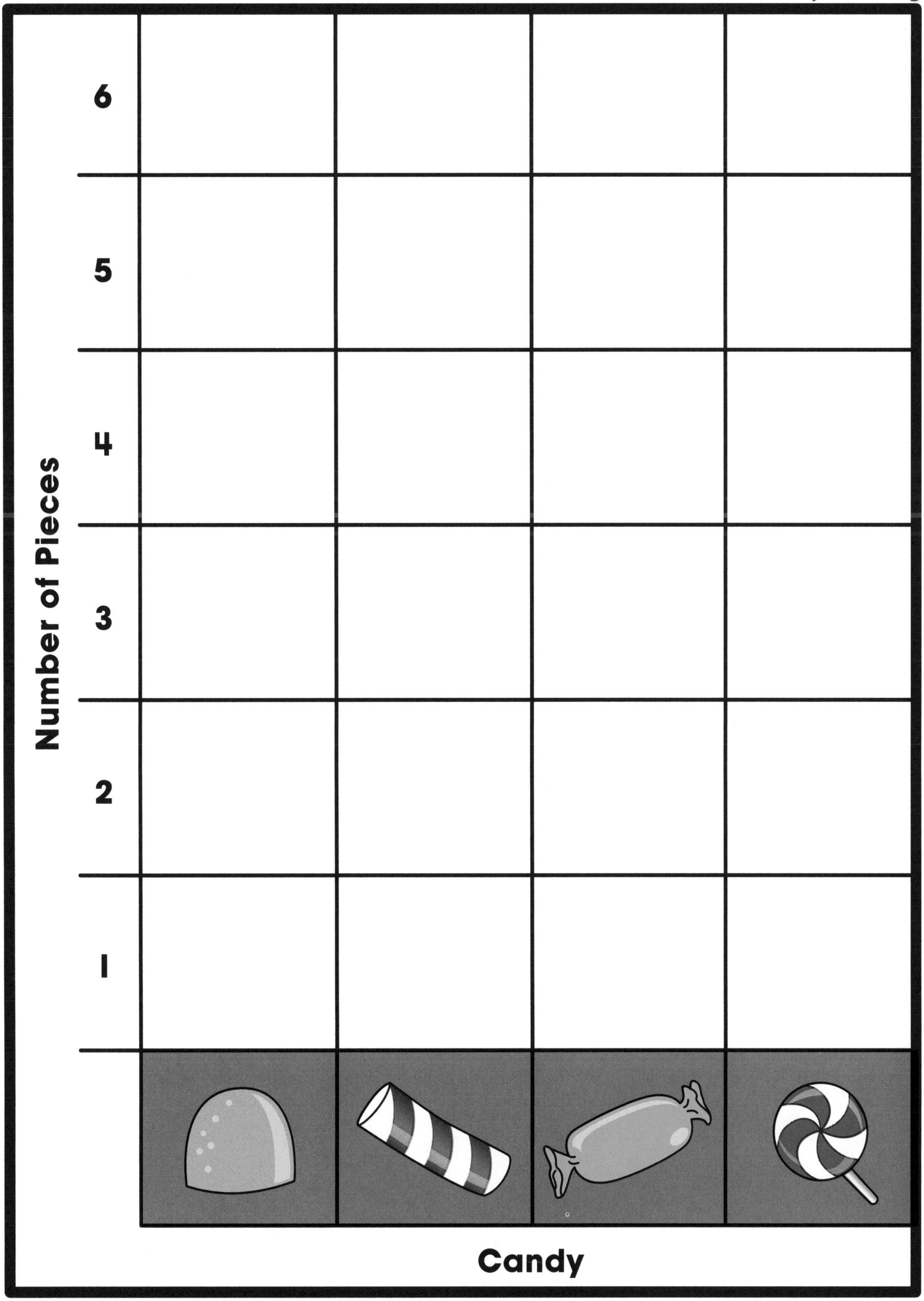

6				
5				
4				
3				
2				
1				

Number of Pieces

Candy

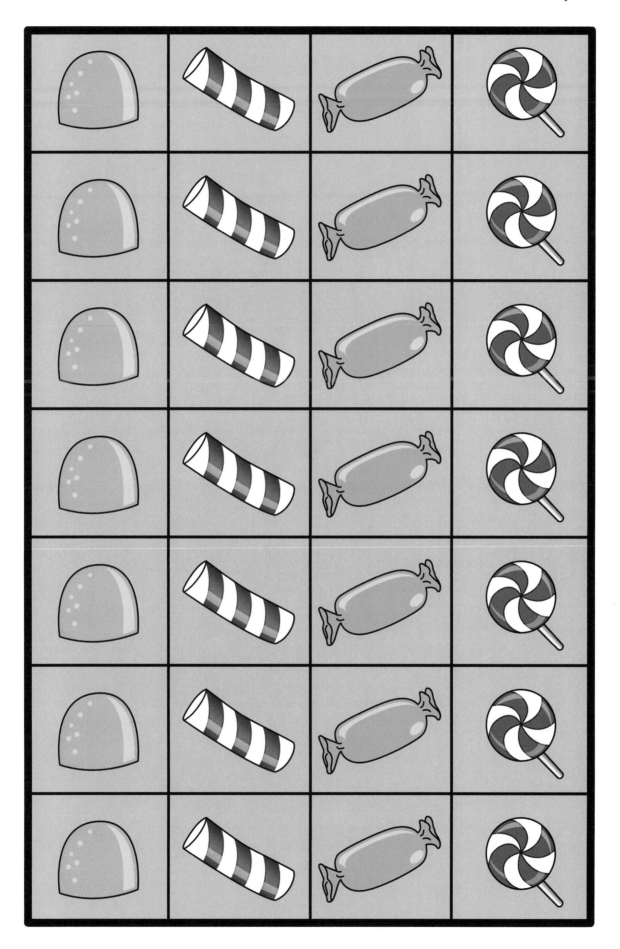

Name_____

Cookie Count

Count each group of cookies. Write the number.

1. _____

2. _____

3. _____

4. _____

Color by Number

Color the correct number of cookies in each cookie jar.

15

20

9

30

Up, Up, and Away

Write the number for each number word in the basket.

Number Match

Draw a line between each matching number and number word.

1. 9	**six**
2. 8	**zero**
3. 4	**ten**
4. 1	**five**
5. 7	**eight**
6. 0	**three**
7. 6	**seven**
8. 2	**four**
9. 5	**one**
10. 3	**nine**
11. 10	**two**

Name_____

Count the Jelly Beans

Write the total number of jelly beans on the line.

1. [2] + [2] = _____

2. [3] + [4] = _____

3. [4] + [6] = _____

4. [8] + [1] = _____

5. [6] + [0] = _____

6. [3] + [2] = _____

More Jelly Beans!

Draw how many jelly beans are in each jar. Then, add the jelly beans. Write the answer on the line.

1. 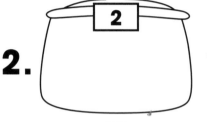 + 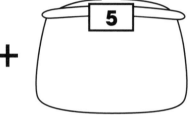 = _____

2. 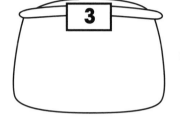 + 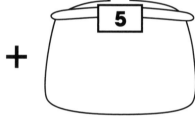 = _____

3. 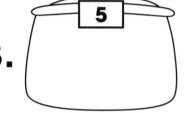 +  = _____

4.  +  = _____

5. 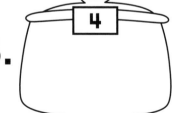 + 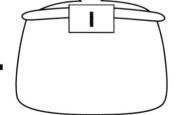 = _____

6. 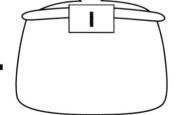 + = _____

Basic Math G.A.M.E.S. • CD-104188 • © Carson-Dellosa

Buzzing About

Write how many bees are left in each set.

1. 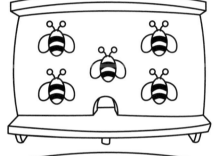 − 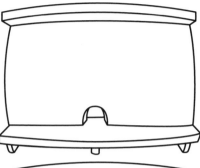 =

2. 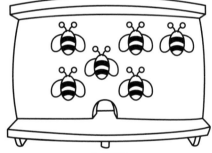 − =

3. 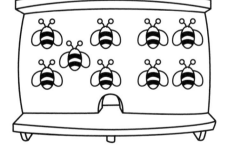 − =

4. 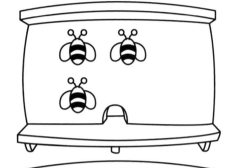 − =

5. 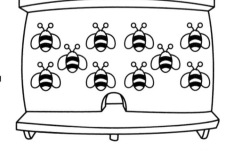 − 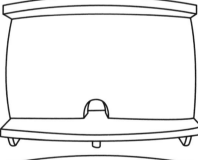 =

Beehive Math

Write the number problem for each picture.

1. 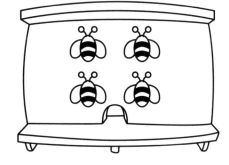 —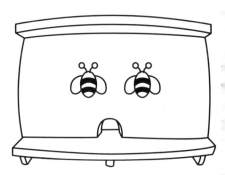

$$\underline{\hspace{3cm}} - \underline{\hspace{3cm}} = \underline{\hspace{3cm}}$$

2. 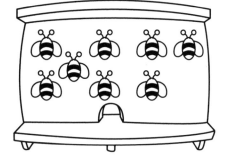 —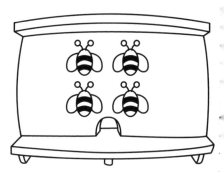

$$\underline{\hspace{3cm}} - \underline{\hspace{3cm}} = \underline{\hspace{3cm}}$$

3.  —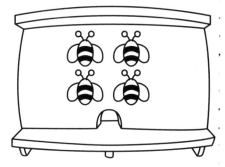

$$\underline{\hspace{3cm}} - \underline{\hspace{3cm}} = \underline{\hspace{3cm}}$$

Doggone Fun!

Circle the word that tells about the picture.

1. **over**   **under**

2. **beside**   **between**

3. **on**   **off**

4. **inside**   **outside**

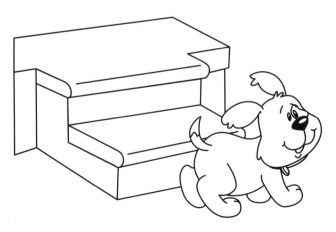

5. **up**   **down**

6. **behind**   **in front of**

Name_____

On My Own

Directional Dog Write the word that tells about each picture.

Word Box

inside	on	under	up

1.

2.

3.

4.

C10

Basic Math G.A.M.E.S. • CD-104188 • © Carson-Dellosa

Shape Up

Draw lines to match the pictures to the shapes.

1.

A.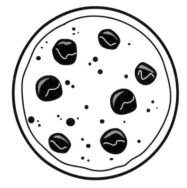

2.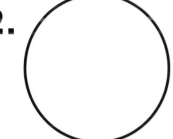

B.

3.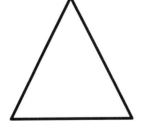

C.

4.

D.

Shape Artist

Draw a picture for each shape.

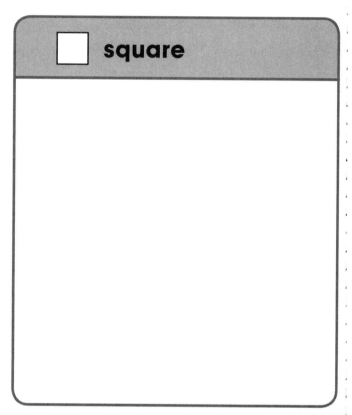

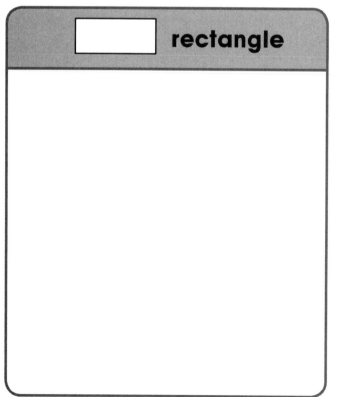

Pretty Patchwork   Finish the patterns.

1.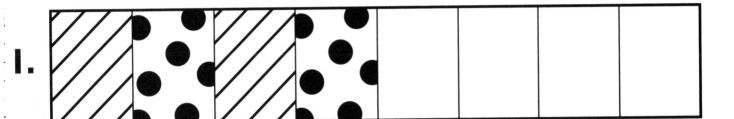

2.

3.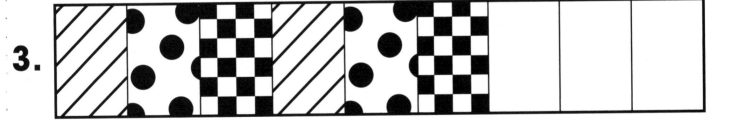

4.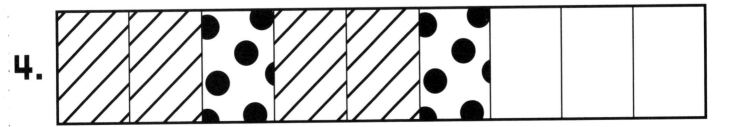

Circle, Circle, Square

Circle the shape that will come next in the pattern.

1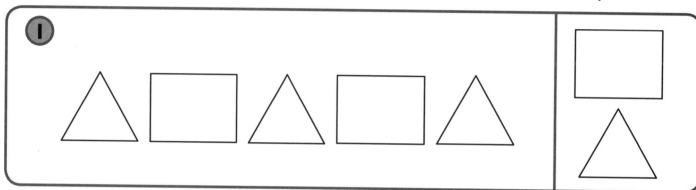

2

3

4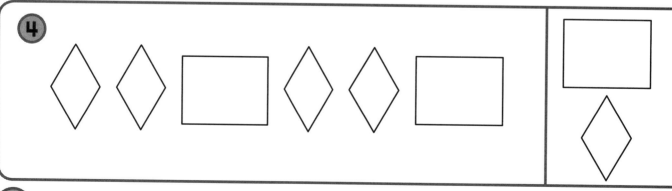

Flower Power

Draw the correct number of flowers in each empty vase. Write the correct number on each vase with flowers.

2

5

6

8

9

Name_____

Apple Count

Circle what comes next in each set.

Basic Math G.A.M.E.S. • CD-104188 • © Carson-Dellosa

Monkey in the Middle

Write the missing number in each set.

Number Box

1	19	16
7	4	10

1
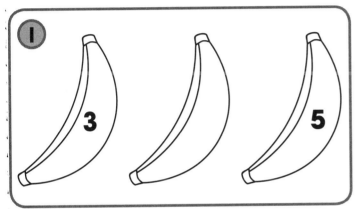
3   5

2
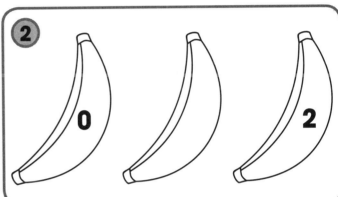
0   2

3
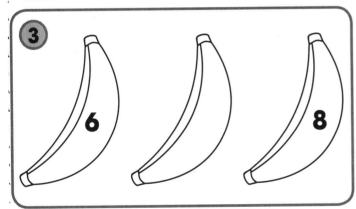
6   8

4
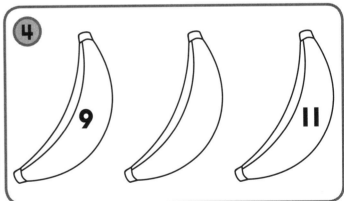
9   11

5
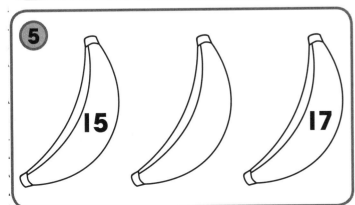
15   17

6
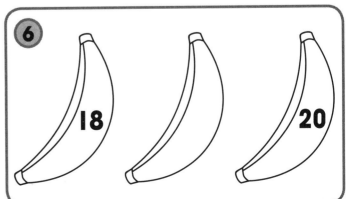
18   20

Number Order

Write the missing number in each set.

1.

2   3   ___   5

2.

9   ___   11   12

3.

13   14   ___   16

4.

___   18   19   20

Gone Fishing

Circle the set with more fish. Draw a triangle around the set with less fish.

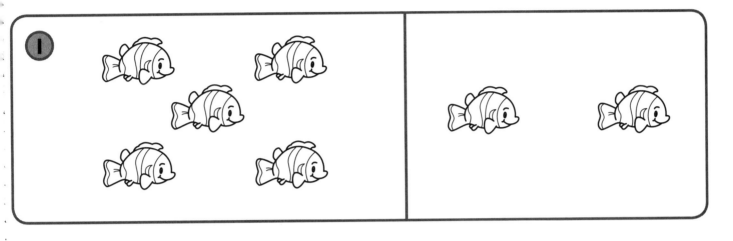

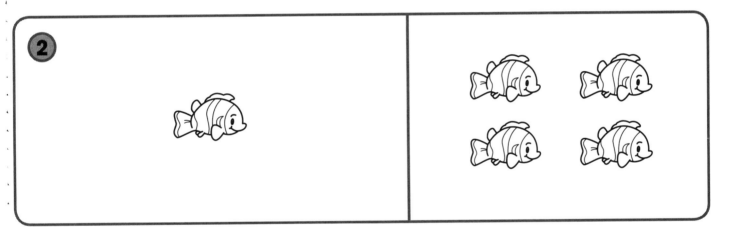

Name_____

More or Less?

Write which set has more.
Write which set has less.

1

_____   _____

- - - - - - - - - - - - - - - -   - - - - - - - - - - - - - - - -

_____   _____

2

_____   _____

- - - - - - - - - - - - - - - -   - - - - - - - - - - - - - - - -

_____   _____

Calendar Cats

Write the missing numbers on the calendar.

Sunday	Monday	Tuesday	Wednesday	Thursday	Friday	Saturday
1	2	3	4		6	7
	9	10		12	13	
15	16			19	20	21
22		24	25		27	
29		31	8 11 5 26			

Name_____

What Day Is It?

Write the day of the
week and today's date.

Today is:

_____

- -

_____

Day of the Week

The:

_____

- - - - - - - - - - - - - -

_____

_____

Date

Word Box			
Sunday	**Monday**	**Tuesday**	**Wednesday**
Thursday	**Friday**	**Saturday**	

Day and Night

Circle the picture that tells
if it is day or night.

1.

2.

3.

4.

Sunrise, Sunset

Draw pictures of things you do during the day and at night.

Spending Spree

Circle the set of coins that matches each picture.

1.

6¢

2.

15¢

3.

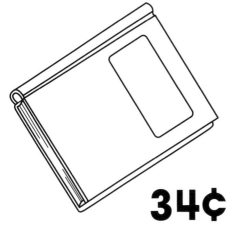

34¢

It Makes "Cents!"

Write the correct number of cents for each set of coins.

1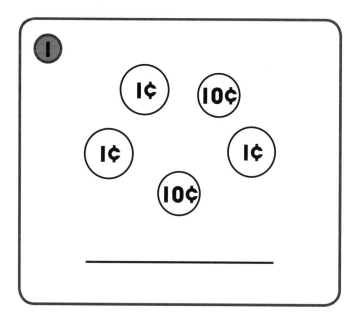

_____

2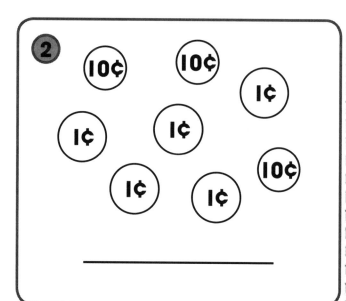

_____

3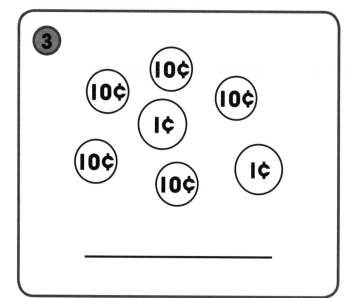

_____

4

_____

Basic Math G.A.M.E.S. • CD-104188 • © Carson-Dellosa

Name_____

Measuring Up

Draw a pencil in each box. Draw one that is long, one that is longer, and one that is longest.

Long

Longer

Longest

Name_____

How Long?

Use a standard paper clip to measure each object. In the box, write about how many paper clips long the object is. Circle the longest object.

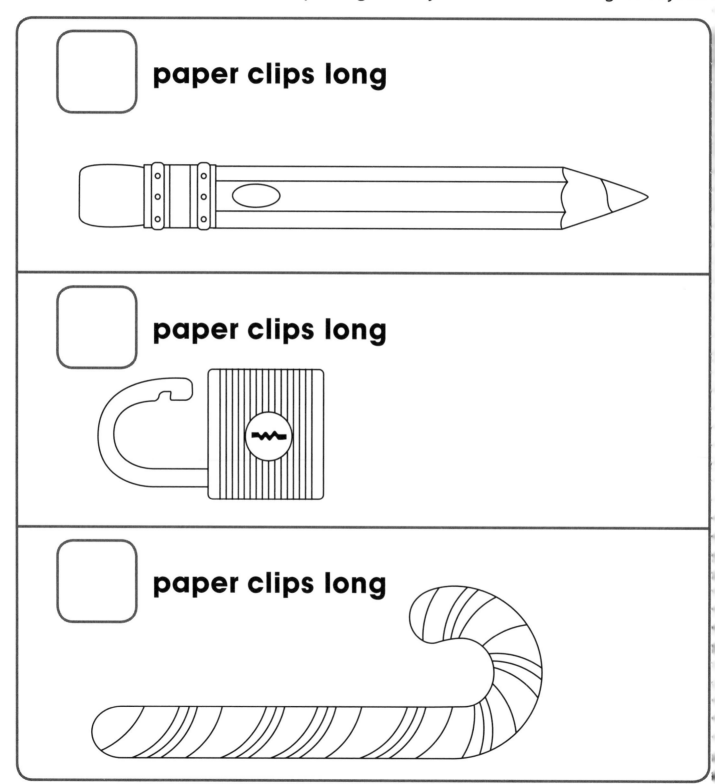

paper clips long

paper clips long

paper clips long

Name_____

Candy Counting

Color a square for each piece of candy in the jar.

Number of Pieces

6

5

4

3

2

1

Candy

Sweet Graph!

Use the graph to count the number of candies.

Number of Pieces

4		
3		
2		
1		

_____   _____   _____

Basic Math G.A.M.E.S. • CD-104188 • © Carson-Dellosa

Answer Key

Cookie Count, C1
1. 17, 2. 20, 3. 28, 4. 30

Color by Number, C2
Students should color the correct number of cookies in each cookie jar.

Up, Up, and Away, C3
From left to right and top to bottom: two: 2; ten: 10; one: 1; four: 4; five: 5; zero: 0; eight: 8; six: 6; nine: 9; seven: 7; three: 3

Number Match, C4
Lines should be drawn between the following numbers and number words:
1. 9, nine; 2. 8, eight; 3. 4, four; 4. 1, one; 5. 7, seven; 6. 0, zero; 7. 6, six; 8. 2, two; 9. 5, five; 10. 3, three; 11. 10, ten

Count the Jelly Beans, C5
1. 4, 2. 7, 3. 10, 4. 9, 5. 6, 6. 5

More Jelly Beans!, C6
1. $3 + 3 = 6$; 2. $2 + 5 = 7$; 3. $5 + 5 = 10$; 4. $3 + 1 = 4$; 5. $4 + 4 = 8$; 6. $1 + 3 = 4$

Buzzing About, C7
1. 1, 2. 4, 3. 5, 4. 5, 5. 7

Beehive Math, C8
1. $4 - 2 = 2$, 2. $8 - 4 = 4$, 3. $7 - 3 = 4$

Doggone Fun!, C9
1. over, 2. beside, 3. off, 4. outside, 5. down, 6. behind

Directional Dog, C10
1. on, 2. under, 3. up, 4. inside

Shape Up, C11
1. C, 2. A, 3. D, 4. B

Shape Artist, C12
Drawings will vary.

Pretty Patchwork, C13
Patterns should continue as follows:
1. diagonal lines, polka dots, diagonal lines, polka dots; 2. diagonal lines, polka dots, squiggly lines; 3. diagonal lines, polka dots, checkers; 4. diagonal lines, diagonal lines, polka dots

Circle, Circle, Square, C14
The following shapes should be circled:
1. rectangle, 2. triangle, 3. circle, 4. rhombus

Flower Power, C15
From left to right and top to bottom, the numbers 1, 3, 4, 7, and 10 should be written on the blank vases. From left to right and top to bottom, 2, 5, 6, 8, and 9 flowers should be drawn in the empty vases.

Apple Count, C16
The following number of apples should be circled: 1. 3, 2. 6, 3. 10

Monkey in the Middle, C17
1. 4, 2. 1, 3. 7, 4. 10, 5. 16, 6. 19

Number Order, C18
1. 4, 2. 10, 3. 15, 4. 17

Gone Fishing, C19

Students should draw circles around the following groups of fish: 1. 5, 2. 4, 3. 8
Students should draw triangles around the following sets of fish: 1. 2, 2. 1, 3. 6

More or Less?, C20

1. less, more; 2. more, less

Calendar Cats, C21

The following numbers should be filled in: 5, 8, 11, 14, 17, 18, 23, 26, 28, 30

What Day Is It?, C22

Answers will vary depending on the date.

Day and Night, C23

The pictures for the following times of day should be circled: 1. night, 2. day, 3. day, 4. day

Sunrise, Sunset, C24

Drawings will vary.

Spending Spree, C25

Students should circle the piggy bank with the following coins: 1. six pennies (six 1¢ coins), 2. one dime and five pennies (one 10¢ coin and five 1¢ coins), 3. three dimes and four pennies (three 10¢ coins and four 1¢ coins)

It Makes "Cents!," C26

1. 23¢, 2. 35¢, 3. 52¢, 4. 15¢

Measuring Up, C27

Students should draw three pencils of different lengths in the correct boxes.

How Long?, C28

1. 5 paper clips long, 2. 2 paper clips long, 3. 4 paper clips long; The pencil should be circled.

Candy Counting, C29

The bar graph should be filled in to show the following information: 4 gumdrops, 1 peppermint stick, 5 wrapped candies, 2 lollipops

Sweet Graph, C30

3 gumdrops, 2 lollipops, 4 wrapped candies